Delicious Medicine
The Healing Power of Food

With 24 Delicious Phyto Recipes for Radiant Health

by Tina "The Medicine Chef" Martini

The Ageless Kitchen

Copyright © 2018 Tina Martini
All rights reserved. This publication may not be reproduced in whole or in part without permission.

deliciousmedicine@icloud.com
themedicinechef.com

ISBN-13: 978-1721895779
ISBN-10: 1721895779

Additional Writing, Editing, Graphic Design and Photo Collage by Glenn Abrams

Special Thanks to the Photographic Community at Unsplash.com

The information in this publication is made available with the understanding that we are not providing medical, psychological, or nutritional counseling services. The information should not be used in place of a consultation with your health care or nutrition professional.

Image of Seeding, Tilling, and Harvesting Maize and image of Ethnobotanic Plants used for Medicine is from the digital edition of the *Florentine Codex* created by Gary Francisco Keller. Images are taken from Fray Bernadino de Sahagún, The Florentine Codex. Complete digital facsimile edition on 16 DVDs. Tempe, Arizona: Bilingual Press, 2008. Wikipedia.com

A page of the *Libellus de Medicinalibus Indorum Herbis* illustrating the Tlahçolteoçacatl, Tlayapaloni, Axocotl and Chicomacatl plants used to make a "remedy for a wounded body" is from an Aztec herbal manuscript describing the medicinal properties of various plants composed in 1552 by Martín de la Cruz and translated into Latin by Juan Badianus. Wikipedia.com

Dedication

To my Grandfather, who shared his love of the garden with me.

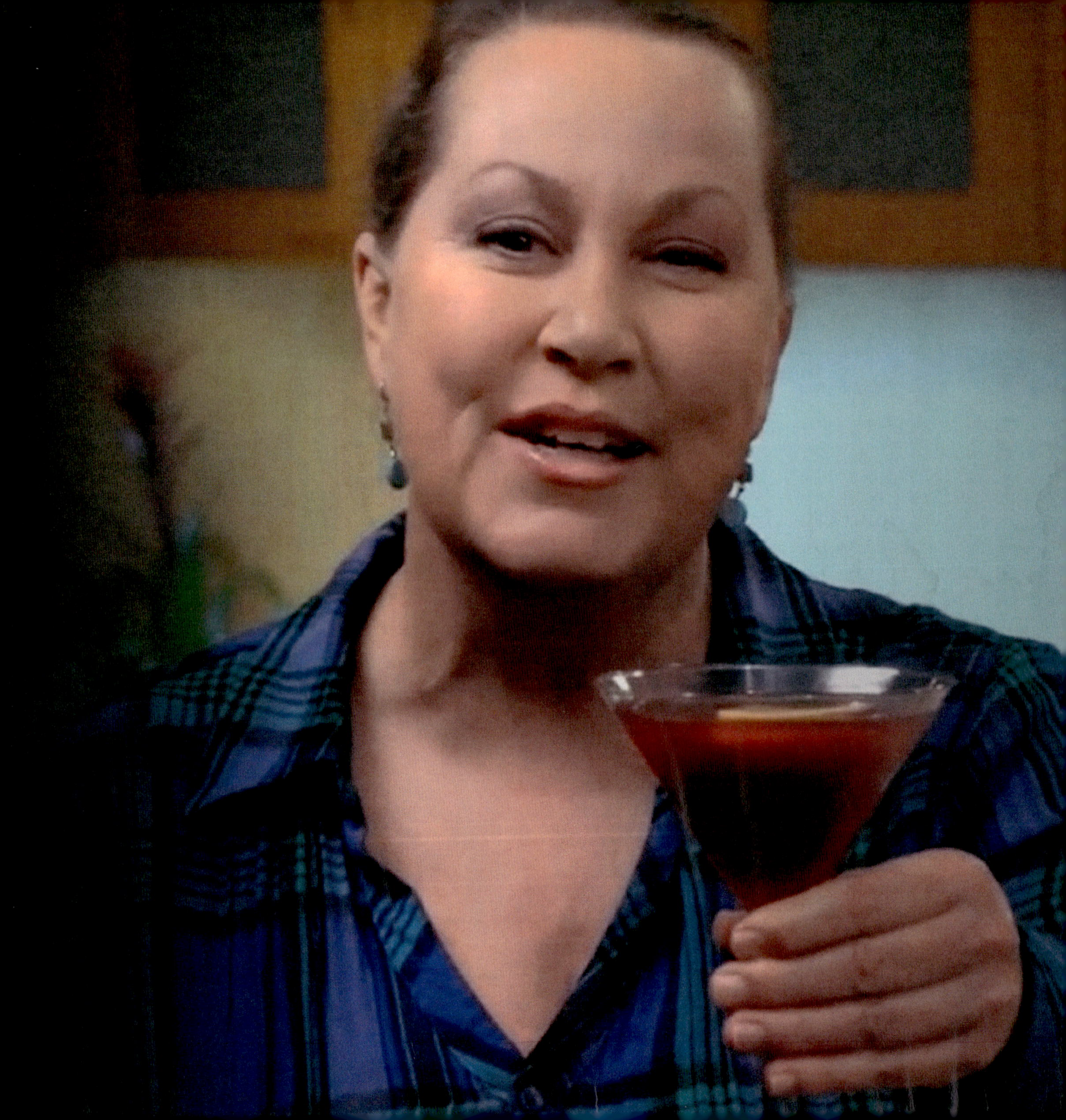

About the Author Tina Martini

Affectionately referred to as **The Walking Encyclopedia of Human Wellness**, Fitness Coach, Strength Competitor and Powerlifting pioneer, **Tina "The Medicine Chef" Martini** is an internationally recognized Naturopathic Chef and star of the cooking show, **Tina's Ageless Kitchen**. As Chef / Owner, at the **Ageless Kitchen** restaurant, Tina's cooking and lifestyle show has reached millions of food and fitness lovers all over the globe.

Over the last 30 years Tina has assisted celebrities, gold-medal athletes and over-scheduled executives naturally achieve radiant health using **The Pyramid of Power**: balancing *Healthy Nutrition* and the healing power of food with *Active Fitness* and *Body Alignment* techniques.

Working with those who have late stage cancer, advanced diabetes, cardiovascular and other illnesses, Tina's clients are astounded at the ease and speed with which they are able to restore their radiant health.

Having served as Educational Chef with **Whole Foods Market**, Tina has also acted as a spokeswoman for the **American Heart Association's Go Red for Women** campaign, and has developed wellness strategies and presented team-building workshops for large corporations, including **PepsiCo, Inc**. She has also designed menus to manage stress and disease prevention for our elite **US Armed Services**.

Tina believes that maintaining balance in our diet, physical activity, and in our work and spiritual life is the key to our good health, happiness and overall well being.

Currently Tina is implementing a new **Cardiovascular Disease Reversal Program** in a university research setting.

Introduction

In this book we'll look at the way a delicious recipe is prepared, share its phyto-nutrient health benefits and healing power, along with some handy hints to help make life more fun and efficient in the kitchen.

Carrots | Jonathan Pielmayer

Chefs,

You may be asking yourself just what is **Delicious Medicine**? And, if it's really medicine, how can it be delicious?

Well, for over 5000 years, scholars and physicians of all beliefs have been telling us that "food is medicine." I just thought it was time we make it delicious, too.

My interest in medicinal nutrition began at the age of eight. I knew instinctively that if food is what grows us, then it's also what heals us.

My first experience with "real food" began with my grandfather; not that my mother didn't feed us real food - she did. But, the magic of the garden was the gift my grandfather gave to me and it has lasted a lifetime!

Pulling fresh carrots out of the dark, rich soil was a treat I looked forward too - even more than my mom's homemade candies. We would wash off the carrots and eat them, standing in the morning sun. I loved that peaceful feeling, and sweet, crisp taste. But more than anything, I loved the time spent with my Granddad.

Fifteen years later, I heard the word *Phytonutrient* for the first time and the puzzle pieces of my life fell together.

I understood from both ancient and modern medicine, that naturally occurring nutrients in plants give fruits, vegetables, grains and legumes their medicinal, disease-preventing, health enhancing properties.

Currently, working with those who have late stage cancer, advanced diabetes, cardiovascular and other illnesses, my clients are astounded at the ease and speed with which they are able to restore their radiant health.

Given the right tools, our bodies can heal from even the most feared diseases.

This is your guide to feeling great again, to having the energy you need to accomplish your dreams, help others, and simply get more enjoyment out of life.

The more we know about what food can do for our health, the more success we will have making lifestyle changes, and the more likely we are to reach our goals.

Welcome to **Tina's Ageless Kitchen!** Reach out if you have questions. I'm so happy you're here!

Tina

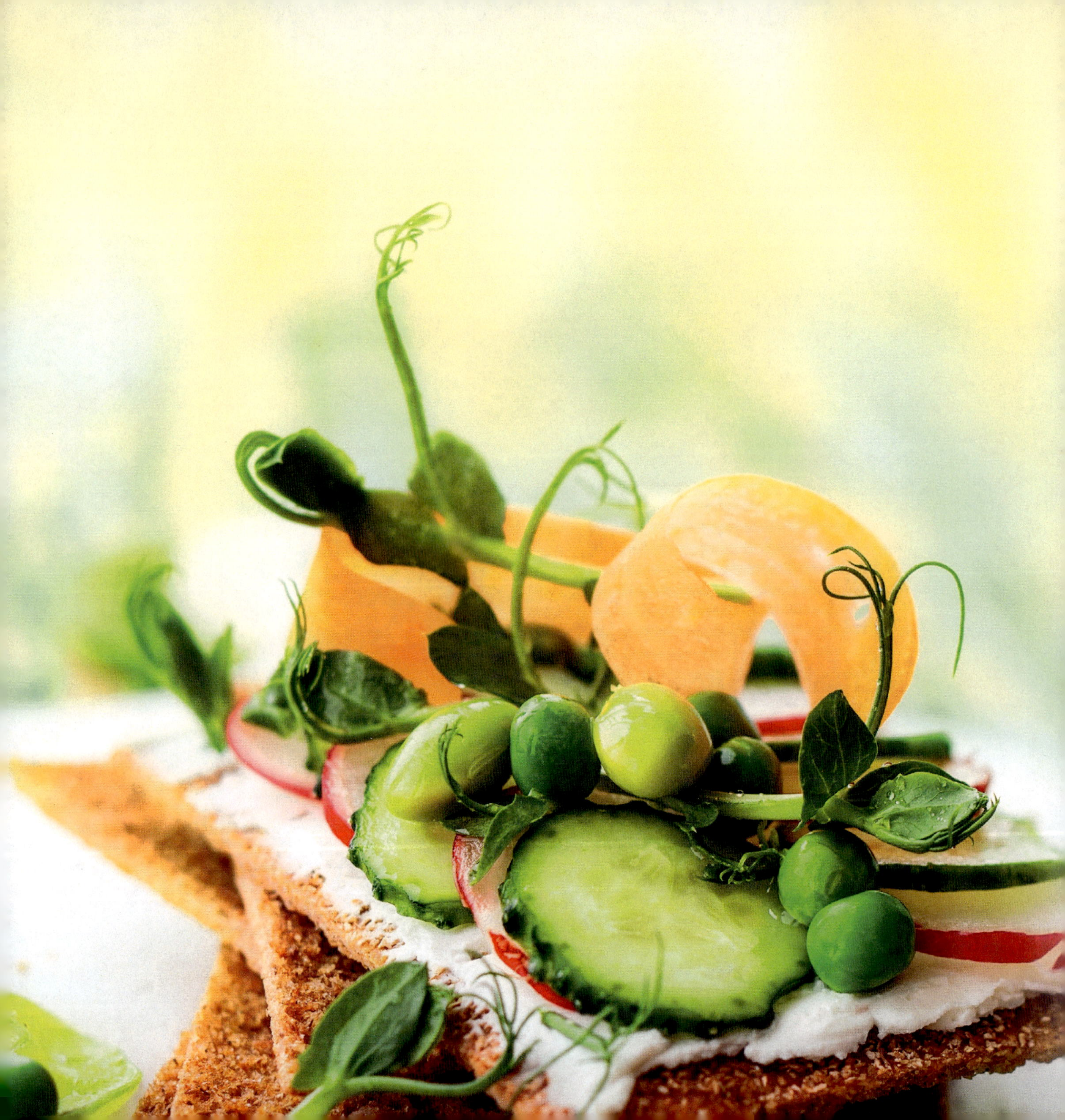

Table of Contents

About the Author Tina Martini

Introduction

Reclaim our Radiant Health — Page 1

Take Control of Your Health — Page 2
- Work / Life Balance
- Active Lifestyle
- Rest & Rejuvenate
- Relationships, Joy & Laughter

Food as Medicine — Page 6
- The History of Medicine
- The Healing Power of Nature
- Food as Medicine in the Kitchen

Phytonutrients — Page 12

Phytonutrient Charts 1 & 2 — Page 14, 16

Creating Your Kitchen Masterpiece — Page 18

Daily Eating — Page 20

Recipe List: 24 Food & Beverage Recipes — Page 22

Bonus - 3 Steps to Disease Prevention — Page 80

Get Shredded - 30 Day Rip Up Plan — Page 82

Alphabetical Recipe Index — Page 88

Donuts | Patrick Fore

Apple | Benjamin Wong

> "Because of my own increased health, wealth and happiness, I am now able to help others live a delightful, interesting and satisfying life of the most widely useful kind. My good - *our good*, is universal."
>
> ~ Rev. Catherine Ponder, *The Pioneer of Positive Thinking*

Reclaim our Radiant Health

How did we get so far away from healthy eating – one of the life's most natural acts?

It's something we have to do every day to survive. It's a way we keep family traditions alive, and a way to keep our bodies healthy and vibrant. Yet, over the past 30 years eating has somehow become a method of torture and condemnation.

A client once said to me, "If I could wake up for just one day and not have my first thought be, 'What am I *not* going to eat today?' I would have a happy life!"

People tend to over-complicate things - to use life's essentials as a reward system - a way to tell us we are loved and valuable. Yet, that's not the purpose of food.

Be well. Be ready.

Food is simply the fuel for our body: the car we drive through life! However, if we take care of our bodies and keep a balanced, healthy lifestyle then we can be happy and well prepared to take care of those around us.

Be well. Be ready. It's that simple! That's our purpose.

Tina Martini

Take Control of your Health

Each of our lives encompass these areas:

Relationships, Health, Career and Spirituality.

And they're all interconnected.

So what does a "Healthy Lifestyle" look like in today's world?

Maintaining **balance** in how much we sleep, eat, exercise, work and relax is very important.

Each of these areas has a direct affect on our health, our happiness and our overall wellness.

A balanced life of movement, rest and nutrition.

2 | Delicious Medicine

Tina Martini

Work / Life Balance to Reduce Stress

Day-to-day stress does more damage to our health and well being than anything else known to man. It causes hormone imbalance, the release of chemicals that cause aging, insomnia, weight gain, aches and pains, depression – the list goes on.

Our life is a gift. Radiant health is your birthright. We are meant to be filled with joy, the spirit of adventure, and childlike wonder. Stress and worry are negative goal setting. We have the ability to overcome these things.

How?

The most powerful way: Balanced Nutrition, Movement and Rest. It's the simplest form of living a peaceful life.

Active Lifestyle

If, for some reason, you were unable to move, you might be pleading and praying just to be active. A balanced, healthy lifestyle includes regular, active movement. Think of movement and exercise as a gift we can give our body. Not as a way to punish ourselves.

Tina Martini

To get started, find some simple activity that you enjoy doing. Then simply do it. Can't get to a gym and need an activity that can be done at home? Do you have a few stairs in your house? A housebound dog?

Humans tend to choose what's familiar, not necessarily what's best for them. If a gentle walk around the block was enough activity to cut your need for medication in half, why wouldn't you start walking? Like anything new, we must be prepared to give ourselves a little more encouragement in the beginning.

Please feel free to email me and I can show you some simple, fun activities that you can do easily - with immediate results.

deliciousmedicine@icloud.com

Reach out, take the plunge. You're not alone! You will be so happy you did.

Rest

ho·me·o·sta·sis

/ˌhōmēəˈstāsəs/

noun

1. the tendency toward a relatively stable equilibrium between interdependent elements, especially as maintained by physiological processes.

Rest is as important as your work. Sometimes more important. In our faster-than-the-speed-of-light society often our minds don't return to the deepest form of rest and recovery - known as homeostasis.

We can't keep our engines revving 24/7 and expect to live a long, healthy life. We are only given so much Chi, or *life force*, when we come into this life. Chugging endless caffeine during the day and then knocking ourselves out with alcohol and sleeping aids at night will not give us more hours in the day. As a matter of fact, we're seeing detrimental results like teenage stroke and heart attacks from over-stimulation.

How can we take so much from our minds and our bodies, and give so little?

Rejuvenate

How do we rejuvenate our minds?

It's often something as simple as finding a peaceful place in your home to clear your mind for 15 minutes.

Yes, this may be difficult at first, but with intention you can master a peaceful mind in the most chaotic environment. Viewing nature is also a quick and effective way to lower blood pressure and release positive, healing hormones in your brain and body.

Simple Action Step

Take a few minutes before you eat your lunch to write down two thoughts, feelings and / or emotions that have occurred during your morning. Put the paper away and then review it at the end of the day. This activity can help "clear" our thought pattern. You can also look at the events of the day more objectively and then take any corrective actions necessary.

Turning off your electronic devices ninety minutes before bed and gazing at a flickering candle flame helps prepare us for deep, healing sleep. It calms and restores the nervous system and awakens creativity and intuition.

In this highly competitive world many top CEOs use these rejuvenation techniques to help make insightful business decisions and to hone their intuitive edge.

Relationships, Joy & Laughter

When is the last time you really laughed so hard you couldn't stop? A real belly laugh that made your cheeks hurt?

Racing toward the finish line steals our joy. Look at kids, or those people who aren't busy making plans. They joyfully take life as it comes.

Now, we don't want to get too crazy with our "carefree attitude." As adults, we must have some kind of plan or who knows where we may end up. But the flexibility to flow with whatever life gives us has a direct effect on our state of mind, our health and disease fighting ability. Ruminating on the things we can't control only brings frustration and a loss of hope.

Scheduling time to laugh is as important as that staff meeting. It renews your feel-good hormones and our faith that life is good and that we do matter to others.

An added benefit: Laughter also raises your immune system activity!

"If people only knew the healing power of laughter and joy, many of our fine doctors would be out of business. Joy is one of nature's greatest medicines. Joy is always healthy. A pleasant state of mind tends to bring abnormal conditions back to normal." ~ Rev. Catherine Ponder

Food as Medicine

The History of Medicine

The true origin of medicine is hard to define. A manuscript from the 16th century illustrated herbal plants **The Aztecs** used to create a *"remedy for a wounded body"*.

Many feel the **Chinese** were the first physicians and pharmacist - having discovered medicinal herbs over 2000 years ago, while India's **Ayurvedic** Medicine is documented to be well over 5000 years old with accounts of medical knowledge being transmitted first from the Gods, then to Sages and then to human physicians.

It seems every culture has a protocol for helping and healing, either by harnessing the natural healing power of nature, or connecting to a power greater than ourselves.

This is how medicine began.

And the common thread:

The Healing Power of Nature

We know that simply engaging with nature can lower the blood pressure and calm both our nervous system and brain chemistry. But, did you know that conventional medications got their start in the flower fields?

Take the heart stimulate medication *Digitalis* - it is made from the dried leaves of the beautiful *Foxglove* flower. *Aspirin* comes from the bark of a *Willow tree*. Calendula and Arnica are medicinal plants used in ointments and topical treatments for bruising and skin irritations.

Edible Medicine.

Aztecs, Incas, Mayans, Toltecs

These ancient Mesoamerican civilizations so revered the creations of nature that they included grains in their sacrificial rituals.

These ancient athletes and architects who felt they were divinely inspired to build and run, sought energy of a different kind, relying on powerful grains and seeds, like **Chia**, to provide protein and complex carbohydrates for day to day activity, as well as long term endurance required for ritual ball sport and battle.

Corn Field | Eric Fleming

Maize, packed with many powerful phytonutrients, was their number one crop. The Aztecs tell of an ancient God and a red ant who were searching for the ideal food to give to humankind and chose to deliver a piece of this most precious grain to the very first human beings.

Seeding, Tilling, and Harvesting Maize | The Florentine Codex

The other top healing foods for civilizations who revered strength and endurance: **Cacao**. It was a favored drink flavored with chili peppers, honey, spices and herbs. Prized for giving energy, it was considered to be a gift from The Gods.

Large, hearty **Squash** varieties, **Quinoa, and Avocados** - all plant based foods high in minerals and Amino acids.

Wild Game was served only when the hunt was successful. In almost every culture, preserved meats and fish were served mainly in Winter. Meat is considered a Fire Food: used to warm the body.

Ethnobotanic Plants Used for Medicine | The Florentine Codex

Tina Martini   Delicious Medicine | 7

Ancient Chinese

The Acupuncture TCM (Traditional Chinese Medicine Physician) treated the whole being using structured exercise, massage, and medicinal nutrition - a prescription for a full and energetic life.

Naturopathy as we know it today - treating or preventing disease through diet, exercise and massage - has its roots in Traditional Chinese Medicine.

食物是医学

In Traditional Chinese Medicine, the foods you ingested were analyzed for their life-giving, energetic quality. One wouldn't consume "dead food" and expect to raise their Chi, or life-force. All foods were selected for the patient based on the season and the current physical condition and emotional experiences of the one seeking relief. As in Ayurvedic Medicine, we see extensive use of fermentation as a great way to preserve food, and in general, provide the ability and power to preserve the life force. Acupuncture TCM protocol also utilized many types of roots, like Ginger - known for its digestive healing, as well as spore-bearing fungus like mushrooms, each with its specific healing and sacred spiritual properties.

Ayurveda आयुर्वेद

Ayurveda is one of the oldest systems of medicine, if not the oldest. The Ayurvedic practitioner has a very common-sense approach to treating the whole person based on the three **Doshas**, or body types. All of us come into this life with a biological nature or body type. For example, perhaps you or a friend have an A-type personality, can eat anything and never gain weight, always fidget and can never sit still. These people have the **Vata** body type. Vata means "The Wind." The other two body types are: **Pitta** (Fire), and **Kapha** (Water).

Ayurveda literally translates to 'The Science of Life', and specific food selection is essential for the Ayurvedic Physician to create an optimal balance of the three Doshas. The other consideration is the six Rasas, or tastes: Sour, Salty, Sweet, Bitter, Pungent, and Astringent. Ideally, by including all six tastes in an Ayurvedic diet, a person would be nourished and satisfied.

Lemons, Ghee (Clarified Butter,) and Curry spices, are considered serious medicine and have a spiritual place in India's culinary culture. Specific herbs, as well as fermented full-fat dairy help to cleanse and tone the digestive system. Colorful fruits and vegetables are to be included in every meal. For every body type, good digestion is important, but nutrient absorption is the ultimate goal.

A plant-rich diet is the foundation for every body type.

Food as Medicine in the Kitchen

Today, there are many opinions about what we should eat, how much we should eat, and when we should eat it. However, in my 31 years as a health supportive chef, and my 39 years in the fitness industry, I have discovered that it is **balance** in all areas of life that maintains and enhances radiant health – preventing disease and restoring us in times of illness – no matter how severe.

No Diets / No Fads

In the short term, we've seen some people make some diets work, but over a lifetime, more than anything, a healthy lifestyle comes from three things:

1. Examining the way we see food and its purpose
2. The amount of sleep we get.
3. The activity and movement in our life.

For example, if we have had major changes in our life, often it will first show up on our bodies and in our emotional health. Honestly, do any of us still run around the way we did when we were kids? Think of the "Freshman 15." The weight gain associated with starting college. We went from running around every day, to sitting around studying. We're bound to experience a change in our metabolism, as well as the ever changing landscape of the human hormone profile.

Keeping our hormone receptors healthy (whether we are male or female, age 12 or 64) has a lot more to do with maintaining consistency and balance in whatever we're doing to improve our overall wellness rather than partaking in yo-yo dieting or following the latest food fads.

"Food First" Lifestyle
Prioritize Your Time

One of the first steps to radiant health is making a commitment to an active and "Food First" lifestyle. One of the biggest challenges we face is finding the necessary time to both buy and prepare healthy food, as well as being active. Ask any sales representative who works in a gym, and they will tell you *not-enough-time* is the biggest objection they face, and the most time-restricted people are the moms - the person with her finger on the pulse of her family's nutritional needs.

Family Activity: Meal Prep Day!

Choose one day per week for the whole family to participate meal planning and food prep for the week. It's something that will have a surprisingly positive effect on your communication, budget and family health. Have each person contribute a dish idea and a shopping list. Work together. Step outside the usual menu and encourage each team member to contribute during all steps of the process. You may find hidden kitchen talent just waiting to be discovered!

As I always tell my up-and-coming young cooks:

"Cooking is a team sport - and fine food is in the details."

Tina Martini

"The intelligent person, remembering the pain of disease, should take food which is suitable to him, and in its proper quantity and timing."

~ Charaka   *India's "Father of Medicine"*

"The food you eat can either be the safest and most powerful form of medicine, or the slowest form of poison."

~ Ann Wigmore   *The Mother of the Raw Foods Movement*

Growing your Own Food

Home grown food provides fresher, tastier and often more nutritious fruits and vegetables - plus you'll know what kinds of fertilizers or pesticides have come in contact with your food.

Growing your own food is time well spent, with a great reward. Almost every city, county, or town has a **community garden** of some sort. If you can't find a community garden, check with schools and churches in your area, or talk to the vendors at your local farmers market.

Suffer from depression, loneliness and Detachment Syndrome?

Get in the dirt... plant one plant... start somewhere. Soon you'll be hooked on the healing power of growing your own food!

Phytonutrients #DeliciousMedicineChest

Phyto is the Greek word meaning plant.

Phytochemicals, known as **Phytonutrients**, are naturally occurring chemicals in plants that give fruits, vegetables, grains, and legumes their medicinal, disease-preventing, health enhancing properties.

The recipes in this book are based on the Phytonutrient benefits provided by each of their ingredients.

The benefits provided by these nutrients are listed on the **Phytonutrient Charts** that follow, and provide a good foundation into all of the delicious medicine available in our food.

Eating a wide variety of foods each day ensures that we receive a broad range of the vitamins, minerals and phytonutrients that our bodies need to stay healthy and help prevent disease.

Tina Martini

Organic Colorful Heirloom Tomatoes | Vince Lee

Delicious Medicine | 13

Phytonutrients Chart #DeliciousMedicineChest

Source	Benefit	Phytonutrient
Broccoli, Bok Choy, Cabbage, Cauliflower and Radishes	Prevents and treats hormone-based cancers: Prostate, Cervical, Breast and Lung.	Indole-3-Carbinol Sulforaphane
Wasabi, Dark Leafy Greens	Boosts the body's natural cancer fighting enzymes.	Isothiocyanates
Soy, Cabbage, Whole Grain, Flaxseed, Legumes, Lychee Fruit, Passionfruit and various types of Berries	Prevents and treats arthritis and asthma, relieves premenstrual and menopause symptoms, prevents osteoporosis and regulates mood.	Phytoestrogens Genistein, Daidzein Enterolactone and Lingans
Fresh Fruits in general. Green Apples and Pears are highest, Aronia berry	Treats diabetes and high blood pressure.	Pectin Fiber
Chili Peppers and Horseradish	Lowers cholesterol, relieves arthritis pain and inflammation, stimulates metabolism and helps to detoxify the liver.	Capsaicin Isoflavonoids

Purple & Green Plant | Filip Pizi

14 | Delicious Medicine   Tina Martini

Source	Benefit	Phytonutrient
Dry Beans, Oats, Oat Bran and Fruit	Regulates the pancreas and strengthens the intestines.	Soluble Fiber Lingans
Blueberries, Peanuts, Grapes (with seeds), Cranberries	Lowers cholesterol, fights tumor development and progression.	Resveratrol
Soybeans, Cabbage	Regulators that protect hormone receptors.	Isoflavonoids
Citrus, Tea, Red Wine, Apricots, Blackberries, Black Currants, Broccoli, Camu Camu, Cantaloupes, Cherries, Bilberry and Grapefruit.	Lower cholesterol and strengthens cardiovascular system.	Bioflavonoids
Tomatoes, Watermelon, Pink Grapefruit, Apricots, Pomegranate, Strawberries and Raspberries	Prevents and treats hormone based cancer, prevents heart disease and reduces sun damage.	Lycopene Ellagic Acid

2

Phytonutrients Chart #DeliciousMedicineChest

Source	Benefit	Phytonutrient
Onions, Garlic, Shallots, Leeks, and Chives	Inhibits growth of cancer cells, protects against stomach and colorectal cancer and lowers cholesterol.	Allium Compounds
Citrus Fruit - pulp, white pith and membranes contain the highest amount.	Potent tumor fighter, inhibits blood clots, has anti-inflammatory properties.	Limonene
Acai, Evening Primrose, Borage, Black Currants and cold water fish - Salmon	Stabilizes connective tissue in the skin, promotes firm and plump complexion and protects arteries.	Dimethylaminoethanol Omega 3 Fatty Acids
Apples, Nuts, Black and Green Tea, Dark Chocolate, Onions, and Raspberries	Prevents stroke, protects arteries from plaque buildup, protects against cholesterol damage and prevents blood clots.	Catechins Polyphenols
Acai, Blueberries, Cherries, Cranberries, Raspberries, Prunes, Strawberries, Red and Purple Concord Grapes, Pomegranate and Purple Cabbage	Prevents age related mental decline. Treats arthritis symptoms (inflammation and pain), prevents gout, strengthens cardiovascular system, prevents heart disease and cancer.	Anthocyanins

Blueberries | Joanna Kosinska

16 | Delicious Medicine   Tina Martini

Source	Benefit	Phytonutrient
Onions, Broccoli, Apples, Grape Juice, Red Wine and Tea	Prevents clotting disorders, reduces injury and stress-related trauma, prevents cancer of the gastrointestinal tract.	Quercetin
Kale, Collards, Spinach, Beets, Turnip Greens, Green Veggies, Wolfberry, Kiwi, Citrus and Egg	Filters UV rays from the sun and prevents molecular degeneration.	Lutein Zeaxanthin
Celery, Parsley, Herbs and Spices: Basil, Rosemary, Oregano	Reduces anxiety, protects against UV radiation, anti-inflammatory, and may be the cure for ovarian cancer.	Apigenin
Asparagus, Fenugreek, Herbs and Spices	Antitumor and antidepressant activities. The cure for ALS	Sarsasapogenin
Grapefruit, Bergamot, Sour Orange, Tart Cherries, Tomatoes, Cocoa, Greek Oregano, and Beans	Antiestrogenic, cholesterol-lowering and antioxidant activities.	Naringenin

Tina Martini   Delicious Medicine | 17

Creating Your Kitchen Masterpiece

"Don't cook with wine you wouldn't drink."

~ Julia Child, American Chef, Author & Television Personality.

Ingredients

We can't build our Dream House with a plastic screw driver, and we certainly can't master our Kitchen Masterpiece without the freshest, most flavorful and nutrient-rich ingredients we can source.

Sourcing great ingredients is the foundation of every great meal.

Seasonal Selections

Seasonal selections aren't just for the trendy. Seasonal eating is getting our food at the time it naturally grows best, providing the most for your money, and usually tastes best. So be sure to taste each of your ingredients to ensure flavor and freshness. It's just as important as the tasting of your finished dish. We can't expect 5-star dishes if we start with inferior ingredients.

Eating Clean

To benefit from the natural nutrients in food, "Clean" eating is all about selecting the freshest most colorful food available in your area, and for your budget.

Growing your own food is the closest to perfectly clean food I can imagine. The farmers markets are connecting our communities with their local food in seasonal and budget-friendly ways. The asparagus poking through the last dusting of snow, tells the people of Italy, *Spring is here!* We can live that way too. Plant an organic fruit tree in your yard. It will become a family favorite, not only telling the season, but yielding nutritious fruit that tastes delicious, like it should.

Choose to be Well

When Fall comes I know it can be hard to say goodbye to our favorite Summer foods. As a result we're forced to find a variety of alternative foods for our plate. Being engaged with the foods we're eating increases our awareness of exactly what we're putting in our mouths, and the more we know about our food, the less we can be fooled by advertising that isn't always in our best interest *– and the longer and healthier our lives will be.*

Try this experiment to see just how programmed we really are by messages telling us not to be well:

Sit in front of the TV around dinner hour. Just watch and

18 | Delicious Medicine

Tina Martini

listen. How many messages do you receive to eat junk food, take a pill, or sit on the couch and binge watch your favorite show?

If I do have a TV night, I get up and exercise during the commercials. I might do bicep curls during one commercial and duck-walks during the next. On average, that can add up to 18 minutes of exercise per hour. If you're watching with your family, make a game out of it!

Enjoy your ability to move and to choose to be well.

Handy Hint
Having the right tools for the job always makes life easier, too. The good news: kitchen gadgets come in a range of prices. They can be purchased with skill level and easy storage in mind. My most useful kitchen tools include my hand-held juicer, my micro plane, and my hand-held immersion blender.

GMO Free Food

The huge debate continues regarding the use of genetically modified organisms in our foods. There is a huge difference between creating a hybrid fruit by grafting one fruit tree branch onto another, versus the use of Genetically Modified Organisms which can change the entire structure of a plant.

A good example of a GMO food is wheat, which has been genetically modified to withstand the pesticides used in large scale farming. As a result, the natural genetic make-up of the plant is changed so when it's eaten the body doesn't recognize it as healthy food, but rather sees GMO wheat as an invader, triggering the inflammation response, the allergy response, and the nervous system response - as if wheat was a food you are allergic too. Even if you are not.

Organic Food

We don't need any more studies to help up us decide if adding hormones, chemicals, antibiotics, and non-food additives is harming us. Just look at the results. I would venture to say that everyone in the United States knows someone who has had cancer, currently is in treatment for, or has already passed from some kind of cancer. Where did all the diabetes type 2 come from? Sitting too much and eating fake foods? Do you think your great grandparents drank a liter of soda per day?

Even the bloating and constant indigestion caused in some people after eating conventional wheat and wheat products brings on mucus over-production, stomach distress of all kinds, headaches, etc. When our bodies sense an invader, it triggers the *"get it out now"* response. Our addiction to antacids and nasal sprays are also connected. In response, the **Gluten Free** food movement is the largest food movement ever seen.

Food labeled as **Organic** *is third-party certified and is shown to consistently contain up to 30% more nutrients because organic farmers tend to the soil first and foremost. It also gives us the best possibility of avoiding foods with residual pesticides.*

Handy Hint
Set up your clean dish area right away. This is part of your "Mise-en-Place." Have your hot/soapy water ready. If you zest a lemon or measure flour into a small mixing bowl; wash it right away and put aside to air dry. It saves you room in the dishwasher for the really dirty dishes.

Daily Eating

We seem to be bound to the idea that breakfast is bacon and eggs, cereal, or an expensive cup of coffee. Or, nothing at all... Seriously? We're still skipping breakfast?

In Japan, a typical breakfast is 6-8 ounces of miso soup, with fresh Ginger, Green Onions, and a few tiny cubes of fresh, organic tofu.

The other night, I had a bowl of assorted olives, goats milk Feta, roasted red bell peppers, and a baked Yam with Curry powder and a drizzle of raw honey. Yup! That was dinner!

Portion Size Matters:

The only common thread in people who enjoy a long, healthy life: **Calorie Restriction.**

Breakfast

If you're in a time crunch, then make a Jaeger Bomb smoothie, or if it's a leisurely morning, put a Cranberry Chia Oat Parfait together, or make some Raspberry or Blueberry Buckwheat pancakes with a favorite nut cream.

If you're going to indulge in a higher fat meal or foods that are harder to digest; this is the time to do it.

Never over-stuff oneself. I no longer allow myself to overeat. When something is really tasting great, I remind myself that there will surely be another opportunity to taste it again.

Overeating does damage to nerve receptors in the stomach, colon and brain, and also reduces production of the fat burning protein, **Leptin**.

Delicious Medicine — Tina Martini

Figure | Todd Desantis

Lunch

Lunch should be the largest, most nutrient dense meal of the day. Greens are a good choice, due to their cleansing ability, and antioxidant-rich profile.

Grains and Greens together are a satisfying and energizing mid-day meal. Protein is more difficult to digest and can make us feel sleepy, so no more than 4 ounces of protein would be recommended for lunch.

Top your Grain and Green bowl with dried fruit and toasted nuts. **Food with Phyte!**

That should send you back to work with ambition to complete your mission!

Dinner

Lighten up after a long, busy day. Keep your motor running efficiently, as you settle in for a movie and some much needed couch time.

Small portions of your favorite comfort foods, can actually help produce more **Serotonin**, our sleep inducing hormone. A healthfully prepared whole grain macaroni and cheese, a flatbread with veggies and some spice will kick that metabolism up one more time before we enter deep, healing, reparative sleep.

Always drink water in the evening, as you lose at least a pint during sleep while you're doing your healing work. Stay with it, and your bladder will calm down and adjust to the wonderful new routine.

Again, don't feel obligated to the traditional dinner.

Snacks

We've heard that we should eat six small meals per day. And it really is the best way to keep our nutrient stores full, our mental health balanced, and our metabolism set - not only to burn fat, but fight off disease.

Grazing on small, nutritious meals wins every time.

The French have a way of eating that is based on the theory that we aren't tasting anything after the first three bites: so, why continue to eat?

Again, balance your hunger, just like everything else in your life. A snack should be just enough to keep you from devouring everything in your path on the way home from work: Three Bhakti Bites, a small apple with some nut butter. A hard boiled egg with a little raw veg.

Get out of the baby carrot box, please. Change it up every day for maximum nutritional benefit.

Eggs | Katherine Chase

Delicious Medicine | 21

Food and Beverage Recipes

GF = Gluten Free
V = Vegan

All of the recipes in this book are both delicious and supportive to your health and can be modified to meet your personal preference. Feel free to substitute ingredients as you desire.

V GF Cranberry-Orange Chia + Oat Parfait	Page 24
V GF Tofu French Toast with Cherry / Orange Compound Butter	Page 28
V GF Jaeger Bomb Smoothie	Page 30
V GF Fast and Easy Cream of Broccoli Soup	Page 32
V GF Grilled Chilled Peach Soup	Page 34
V GF Asparagus Quinoa with Lemony Vinaigrette	Page 36
GF Asian Shrimp Salad	Page 38
V Jeweled Salad & Creamy Key Lime Dressing	Page 40
V GF Warm Spinach Salad with Coconut "Bacon" Vinaigrette	Page 42
GF Peach Glazed Salmon	Page 44
GF Jerk-Spiced Turkey Burgers with Mango Salsa	Page 46
V GF Stuffed Bell Peppers with Sweet & Sour Tomato Sauce	Page 48
V GF Mini Street Tostadas w/ Black Bean Hummus & Citrus Salad	Page 52
GF Tequila-Lime Chicken and White Chili	Page 54

A Celebration of Nuts, Seeds and Dried Fruit		Page 56
V GF Bhakti Bites: Almond/Coconut, Tahini Vegan, Peanut Butter		Page 58
V GF Nut and Seed Creams - Sweet and Savory Cashew		Page 60
V GF Cashew Cream Mini Frozen "Cheesecake"		Page 62
V GF Gluten Free Pizza Crust and Tomato Sauce		Page 64
V GF Gluten Free Flax Crackers		Page 68
GF Garden Flavored Goat Cheeses		Page 70
V GF Mint Scented Pineapple/Cucumber Granita		Page 72
V GF Buttermilk Dumplings with Warm Blueberry Compote		Page 74
V GF Mulled Wine		Page 76
V GF Chia Hot Chocolate with Coconut Whipped Cream and Coconut "Bacon" Sprinkles		Page 78
Bonus: My 3 Steps to Disease Prevention		Page 80
Get Shredded - 30 Day Rip Up Plan		Page 82

Cranberry-Orange Chia + Oat Parfait

Cranberries aren't just for Thanksgiving. Here, we cook fresh cranberries along with steel cut oats. This is a great recipe to get the kids into the kitchen and have them help make the Chia pudding. In the morning, they'll find a creamy pudding surprise, as the Chia seeds will be in "full bloom". Also soaking the oats overnight speeds their cooking and enhances their creamy texture.

Here's to your family's health, and to fun in the kitchen!

Chia Pudding

- 1/4 Cup Chia Seeds
- 1 Cup Milk, your choice
   I use 1/2 Cup Almond and 1/2 Cup Coconut.
- 2 Tsp. Sweetener, your choice
   I like maple syrup or raw honey.
- 1/2 Tsp. Vanilla
- Pinch of good quality Salt
   I use Pink Himalayan Salt

The night before:
Mix the Chia ingredients together in a jar. Chill overnight.

¼ : 1 is the ratio of Chia to liquid. By selecting other liquids you can use your imagination to create a variety of pudding flavors. Chocolate almond milk is so good!

Oatmeal

- 1 1/2 Cups Water
- 2/3 Cup Steel Cut Oats
- 1/3 Cup Fresh Cranberries
- 2 Tsp. Orange Zest
- 3/4 Tsp. Ground Cinnamon
- Pinch of Salt
- 2 Tbsp. Fresh Orange Juice
- 2 Tsp. Honey or Coconut-Palm Sugar
- 1 Small Can of Mandarin Oranges, drained - *Organic only, please. No BPA. (See pg. 55)*
- 1/3 Cup Toasted Almonds

In the morning:
Bring the water to a boil. Keep a whisk moving and stir in the oats, cranberries, zest, cinnamon, and salt. Cook for the time directed on the package. The cranberries will burst, and the oats should be tender. Remove from heat, stir in fresh orange juice and honey. Allow to rest 5 minutes while you get your parfait glasses, mandarin oranges, almonds, and Chia pudding into an assembly line.

Layer into a parfait glass, starting with a spoonful of the cooked oats, alternating with Chia pudding, a few mandarin orange segments, nuts, and so on. Top with orange segments and a sprinkle of toasted almonds.

Serve immediately.

Tina Martini

Mandarin Oranges

Mandarin Oranges are our greatest weapon against liver cancer. The little segments have thick white veins that contain **Limonene** which inhibits cancer cells from growing. Also high in **Beta Cryptoxanthin**; this phytonutrient helps the body clear Hepatitis C. It also ensures smooth blood flow resulting in lower blood pressure. The Kentucky School of Medicine (these researchers spend their days studying food-as-medicine, only) found that even canned Mandarins where amazingly high in these super-charged anti-oxidants.

If your child is experiencing abdominal distress, vomiting, cramping, or muscular spasms, giving them room temperature Mandarins will stop these symptoms, as well as eliminate any problematic bacteria from taking hold. Start with one segment and go from there. We never want to overload a digestive system in spasm, nor do we want dehydration to set in.

Mandarin juice is loaded with minerals to calm the nervous system during illness. Tangerines of all types are skin care from the inside out. Want to erase crows feet? Mandarins are at the top of the list in reversing environmental damage that shows up on our faces.

Tina Martini

Chia Tiny But Mighty

Chia seeds have all of the benefits of other seeds and more!

- *Ratio of Omega-3 to Omega 6 fatty acids are in perfect balance*
- *One of the best sources of plant protein*
- *Provides topical and internal anti-aging skin care*
- *A GI tract cleanser*
- *Alleviates abdominal bloating*
- *Supports pro-biotic growth in the gut*
- *Helps eliminate oxidative stress on cardiopulmonary function*
- *Reverses insulin resistance and dyslipidemia (fatty blood)*
- *Reduces visceral adipose tissue (belly fat) without exercise*
- *Proven in clinical trials to prevent and reverse Type 2 Diabetes*

History

In the ancient Aztecs and Mayan civilizations this little seed was so revered it was used in sacrificial ceremonies and was considered a special fuel for running long distances. In the Mayan language, Chia means **"strength"**.

Nutritional Value

The nutritional value of Chia is amazing. The energy packed into this tiny seed has been harnessed by long distance runners for centuries - Amino acids, Omega 3's in perfect balance, minerals, and fiber. Chia is a *wellness powerhouse*.

Being a member of the Mint family, Chia is high in **Rosmarinic Acid.** This phytonutrient prevents cell damage caused by environmental free radicals. They reduce inflammation, contain essential amino acids and are a great source of **Omega-3 fatty acids**. Also high in **Boron**, this phytoestrogen calms and protects the hormone receptors. It is the essential mineral for strong bones, teeth, and nails. It has an anti-fungal effect from the inside out, and assists with our toenail and foot health. Boron also increases our uptake of **Calcium, Manganese,** (the craving crusher mineral,) **Magnesium, and Phosphorus**. These minerals build bone and muscle mass.

Chia also prevents and treats both breast and cervical cancer. It prevents tooth decay and bad breath by protecting our teeth from plaque buildup via the Zinc it contains.

Endurance

Sustain your endurance during extra tough workouts when you drink 8 ounces of a Chia-based drink one hour before you train.

26 | Delicious Medicine

Detail, Chia Seeds | Keegan Fields

Tina Martini

Blooming Chia

To avoid accidentally choking on dry Chia, seeds should be hydrated before consumption. Place dry Chia seeds into water or other liquid for approximately 20 minutes, or until the seeds are soft and gelatin-like.

Drinking bloomed Chia gives us a sustained satiety, assisting us in reducing our caloric intake without feeling deprived, and can gently relieve constipation without causing bowel distress or diarrhea.

Baking and Sautéing

Chia can act as a leavening agent in gluten-free baking. You can also use bloomed (pre-soaked) Chia seeds to sauté veggies, meats, and fish. They contain good fat and perform just like any sautéing oil, without the addition of higher-calories.

Wow! All that and more from this tiny #Farmacy.

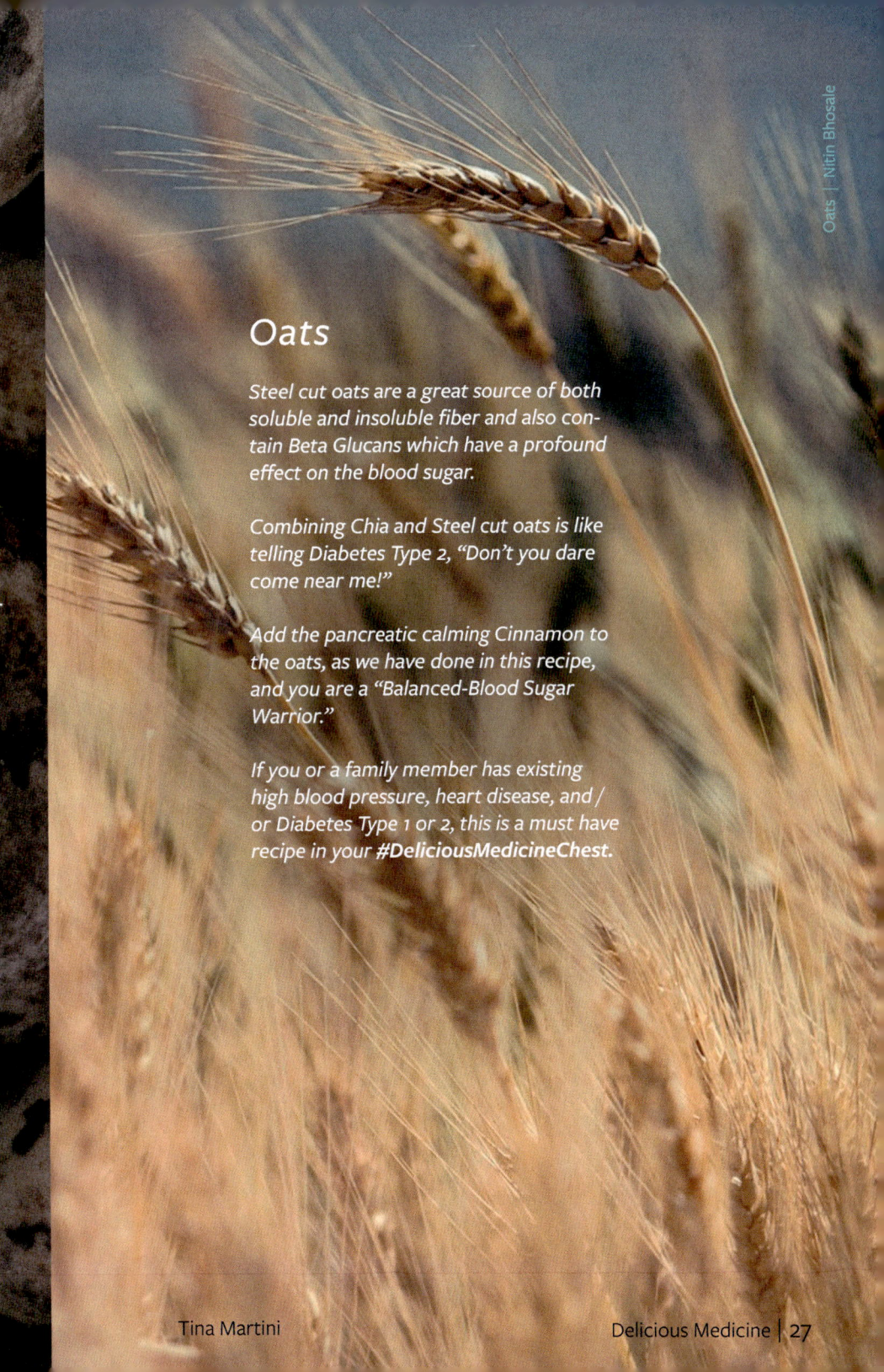

Oats

Steel cut oats are a great source of both soluble and insoluble fiber and also contain Beta Glucans which have a profound effect on the blood sugar.

Combining Chia and Steel cut oats is like telling Diabetes Type 2, "Don't you dare come near me!"

Add the pancreatic calming Cinnamon to the oats, as we have done in this recipe, and you are a "Balanced-Blood Sugar Warrior."

If you or a family member has existing high blood pressure, heart disease, and / or Diabetes Type 1 or 2, this is a must have recipe in your #DeliciousMedicineChest.

Oats | Nitin Bhosale

Tina Martini

Tofu French Toast with Cherry / Orange Compound Butter *Serves 4 to 6*

Tofu makes amazingly rich custards and absorbs flavors like a sponge. This twist on a classic recipe was developed back in 1992, earning me the nickname, **Tofu Guru**. Most people who taste this recipe see no need to return to an egg-battered French toast.

As always chefs, use this recipe to inspire your own signature French toast flavors!

Bread of your choice - I like to use cinnamon-raisin

Cherry/Orange Compound Butter

- 1 Stick Unsalted Butter, room temperature, or Earth Balance Vegan "Butter"
- 2 Tbsp. Dark Sweet Cherries, finely chopped
- 1 1/2 Tsp. Orange Zest
- 1/4 Tsp. Vanilla

Custard

- 1/2 of a 12.3 oz. Box of Silken Tofu - *I use Mori Nu, extra firm.*
- 3/4 Cup Almond Milk
- 1 Tsp. Vanilla
- 3/4 Tsp. Cinnamon
- 1/2 Tsp. Ground Fennel
- 1/3 Tsp. Cardamom
- 1/3 Tsp. Allspice
- 1 Tbsp. Whole Grain or GF Flour
- 2 Tbsp. Maple Syrup

Preparation

Cherry/Orange Compound Butter

Lightly fold all ingredients together in a bowl. Everybody prefers colorful food! To prevent butter from turning a grayish, purple color, do not over-mix. Scoop completed butter onto parchment paper and roll into a log. Twist ends and refrigerate until firm and ready to serve. You can prepare the butter up to two days in advance.

Custard

Drain tofu thoroughly. Place tofu in blender, along with all remaining ingredients. Blend until smooth. Pour custard into a shallow dish.

Heat skillet or griddle to medium-high heat and coat surface with safflower or coconut oil. Dip bread slices into custard and scrape excess batter off on sides of the dish.

This French toast takes a little longer to cook than a traditional egg French toast. Make sure you're just coating the bread and not really soaking it all the way through.

Lay coated bread on hot surface and leave it alone. It will take four to five minutes to brown and firm up. Turn when the corner of the bread comes up easily and cleanly. Place on parchment lined sheet pan and hold in warm oven.

Serve with compound butter and warm maple syrup.

Phyte Bites

Soy (Tofu) can be a very controversial food because there is so much conflicting information about Soy. Please use your common sense when making the decision whether or not to incorporate Soy into your nutrition plan. Ayurvedic Medicine (the oldest system of medicine known) tells us to eat the foods your mother raised you on. If you were not raised on Soy it's best not to over indulge. One 3-ounce serving 2 to 3 times a week is all that would be recommended.

Please do not eat genetically modified soy ever! Organic Soy products only.

Tofu was developed in Indonesia and gradually made its way across Asia. The cancer rate in these high-Soy diet countries was virtually non-existent until the introduction of commercial fast-foods.

Soy contains two very powerful phytonutrients; **Genistein** and **Daidzein**. These are **phytoestrogens** that actually protect the body's hormone receptors from damage. These receptors look similar to a goal post on a football field. When we eat hormone-laden foods, or have an abundance of unmanaged stress, or a sedentary lifestyle, or drink excessive amounts of alcohol the resulting hormones that naturally occur (yes guys, this means you too,) race through our hormone receptors and overload them. The receptor goal posts become twisted, and the hormones themselves become damaged. The DNA is mis-read, and we end up with a mass of cancerous cells, A.K.A. breast cancer, prostate cancer, lung cancer, (yes, lung cancer is a hormone-based cancer) cervical, ovarian, and uterine cancers.

The aforementioned phytonutrients are found in nature. Here's the part that amazes me: these phyto warriors seek out just the damaged hormone receptors, and "park" on top of them, blocking any further hormones from entering and becoming mis-read DNA, thus protecting you from hormone-based cancers!

Nature is so miraculous. Don't you agree?

Tina Martini

The **spices** we are using are Mother Nature's antibiotics. **Fennel** is a powerhouse of digestive medicine, as well as helping to regulate hormone production and is one of the founding foods in ancient Shamanic medicine.

Cherries contain **Anthocyanins**. They strengthen the vascular walls, keep cholesterol in check, and greatly increase circulation to the feet. They also help us sleep more soundly by deepening our circadian rhythm - our natural sleep/wake cycle.

Maple Syrup is a great source of many minerals such as, **calcium, manganese, iron, and potassium**. Minerals help repair environmental damage in our cells as we sleep. This gift from nature also contains phenolic compounds that are also found in blackberries, tea, blueberries, red wine, and flax seed. Phenolic compounds, A.K.A. **Polyphenols**, prevent stroke, protect arteries from oxidative cholesterol damage, and prevent the formation of blood clots.

One of the most researched polyphenols is Epigallocatechin Gallate, or EGCG. This is the compound most sought after in green tea. We know EGCG improves endothelial blood vessel cell function, thus providing cardiovascular strength and protection from heart attack. It also reduces insulin sensitivity and lowers blood pressure. All of these characteristics together help kick your natural fat-burning inferno into high gear.

Delicious Medicine | 29

Jaeger Bomb Smoothie

This Aerobic smoothie was created and named in honor of Jaeger, one of The **Ageless Kitchen's** favorite Food and Fitness Lovers who is the poster boy of the work / life balance.

Aerobic means "with usable oxygen". For the person who might sit in front of a screen all day, if we're not active our red blood cells go to sleep, becoming stacked like poker chips in our torso, so we can't easily absorb oxygen and burn fat efficiently. The ingredients in this recipe provide a big dose of oxygen.

Burning fat by increasing oxygen absorption, and reducing inflammation is The Jaeger Bomb mission. So, here's to moving – even when you're not moving.

Smoothie

¾ Cup Frozen Pineapple
1 Cup Power Greens Mix
  (*in the produce section*)
1/3 Cup Coconut Water
1/3 Cup Almond Milk
1/3 Avocado, peeled and seeded
2 Tsp. Chia
2 Tsp. Hemp Hearts (seeds)
1 Tsp. Vanilla

Preparation

Place all ingredients in a blender and process until smooth and light green. Stop and scrape the sides down 1 or 2 times.

Our customers comment about how light and airy our smoothies are.

We don't add ice and we blend an extra 1 to 2 minutes.

Phyte Bites

Pineapple is a very powerful anti-inflammatory food due to the enzyme **Bromelain**. The highest concentration of Bromelain is found in the core of the Pineapple.

When I cut up a Pineapple to freeze, I include the core. Slice it in *coins* and toss it in with the other fruit. When you blend it, you won't even notice.

All of the different greens contain different phytonutrients. Change 'em up each week.

Avocado, Chia, and Hemp provide **essential fatty acids** and offer a host of other **vitamins and minerals.**

This is a smoothie with serious Phyte and surprisingly delicious taste!

Pineapple | Tadas Mikuckis

Tina Martini

Fast and Easy Cream of Broccoli Soup *Serves 4*

This is a great way to use broccoli stems. Chefs don't throw anything away, so whenever I clean fresh broccoli, the stems go in the freezer to use later in casseroles and soups - delicious bowls of breast cancer prevention.

Soup

1 Tbsp. Butter or Earth Balance Vegan Butter - *to sauté the onions*
1/3 Cup Yellow Onion, diced
2 Tsp. Dried Basil
1 1/2 Tbsp. Grapeseed Oil
1 1/2 Tbsp. Butter or Earth Balance Vegan Butter
1/4 Cup All-Purpose Gluten Free Flour or Unbleached AP Flour
4 1/2 Cups Water
3 Medium Broccoli Stalks
2 Vegan Chicken Bouillon Cubes
   I use Edward & Sons Not-Chick'n Broth and Seasoning
1 Tsp. Salt
1/2 Cup Heavy Cream - *Vegan option: Simmer to reduce 3/4 cup unsweetened full-fat almond milk down to appx. 2/3 cup*
1/4 Tsp. White Pepper
   White pepper is floral and brings out the broccoli flavor nicely. Black pepper also works if that's what you have on hand.

32 | Delicious Medicine   Tina Martini

Preparation

Soup

Wash and separate broccoli florets into bite sized pieces and set aside. Rough chop broccoli stems.

In a small saucepan, sauté onions in 1 Tbsp. butter until soft and lightly golden. Add basil to pan and cook 30 seconds just to release the aroma. Do not brown. Set aside.

In a stockpot, make your roux. Heat grapeseed oil and butter over medium heat. Whisk in flour and stir until thick and creamy looking. 1-2 minutes. Slowly add water to the roux, whisking to avoid any lumps.

Add broccoli stems, sautéed onions and basil, bouillon cubes, and first round of salt. Bring soup to light boil. Cook 20 minutes, stirring occasionally. Taste.

Add your beautifully manicured broccoli florets, reduce heat to medium and cook 4-5 minutes, or until florets are tender. Turn off heat, stir in cream and season for service.

Phyte Bites

Broccoli has some serious antioxidant properties, in general. **Sulforaphane** is the phytonutrient that gives broccoli its distinctive scent.

You may have noticed that broccoli doesn't smell as strongly as it did 10 years ago. The consumer slowed consumption of broccoli and complained of the smell so much that the agriculture industry decided to breed the odor out of the plant. That odor is the aforementioned Sulforaphane. This phytonutrient is the reason broccoli is thought to be the number one food in the fight against breast cancer. We want the whole house to smell like Sulphur when we cook broccoli!

Broccoli is also very high in **Quercetin**. This prevents clotting disorders, reduces injury and stress related trauma. Quercetin-high foods work really well against hormone-based cancers, and cancers of the gastrointestinal tract.

Fat is required to uptake these phytonutrients. The cream is a great carrier for our phytos, and also is a great source of **Alpha-Lipoic-Acid**, one of nature's most powerful liver cleansers. Bye-bye toxins!

Basil contains **Apigenin**. More hormone balancing magic!

Onions and garlic with their **Allium** compounds are at the top of the cancer fighting list and inhibit the growth of cancer cells.

Tina Martini

Grilled Chilled Peach Soup

What do you do with a plethora of peaches?

Make Peach Soup. Then freeze some for later use in Vinaigrette, a Sauce for roasted meat, or to toss into a Smoothie. This is one of my personal favorites! Even if you get some peaches that are not up to our usual standards, this is a great way to use them. And any excuse to have some bubbles... Count me in!

We top this gorgeous creation with sparkling wine, or champagne.

Peach Soup

½ Cup Crème Fraîche (optional)
2 Tbsp. Coconut-Palm Sugar
8 Peaches, pit removed
1 ½ to 2 Tsp. Chinese Five Spice
2 Tsp. each Lemon, and Orange Zest
¼ Cup each Lemon, and Orange Juice
½ Tsp. Vanilla Bean Caviar
   Seeds and pulp scraped from inside the bean pod.
½ Cup Organic Cranberry Juice Cocktail
   No high fructose corn syrup, please.
½ Cup Honey
½ Cup Water
Chilled Sparkling Wine, your choice

Preparation

Whisk *Crème Fraîche* and Coconut Palm sugar together in a small bowl. Cover and chill until ready to serve.

Heat grill to medium-high heat. Sprinkle peaches with Chinese five spice. Place cut side up on grill grate - or use a grilling basket. Close lid and **grill peaches for 15 to 20 minutes**, or until they start to get soft.

Peaches can also be roasted in the oven. Place peaches, cut side up, on a sheet pan. **Bake at 350 degrees for 20- 25 minutes**.

Mix honey and water in a small sauce pan. Simmer until the honey is dissolved and syrup is slightly thickened. Do not boil. Set aside to cool.

Remove cooked peaches from grill and allow to cool. Put all ingredients into a blender, except the honey syrup. Blend thoroughly and pass through a fine mesh strainer. Then sweeten to taste. Chill until ready to serve.

For restaurant quality service, chill bowls and soup spoons as well. Spoon soup base into chilled bowl, top with ¼ cup sparkling wine. Garnish soup with Crème Fraîche / Coconut Palm sugar.

Tasty Tip

Place spent vanilla pod in your sugar canister or bag. You'll save on vanilla extract and have baked goods that have that "certain something" that no one can quite put their finger on.

Phyte Bites

Antioxidants

We could say that this is an anti-aging soup, with peaches, sparkling wine, citrus, honey, and vanilla. All of these ingredients contain phytonutrients that help increase longevity. Peaches contain **Chlorogenic acid**, a phytonutrient that control's the bodies aging process and reduces inflammation. Another key compound are **Bioflavonoids**. These super-antioxidants repress poor cell formation, combat Atherosclerosis and heart disease in general. They also have a "softening" effect on tissue making them perfect to prevent and stop the progression of diseases like Fibromyalgia, Scleroderma, and Alzheimer's disease. Peach tea can also be very effective in assisting the kidneys with their natural cleansing process.

Bye Bye Heartburn

We've talked before about the serious skincare peaches are; but, here's something I would bet most people don't know about peaches. Peaches are Mother Nature's antacid. To implement this remedy, wash and dry the peaches, chill, remove the skin, and eat the flesh. Bye bye, heartburn!

Asparagus Quinoa with Lemony Vinaigrette

Adding vegetables to whole grains always makes for a hearty side dish that can easily double as an entrée. This recipe is also an easy way to start the transition to a plant based diet, and it's one of my personal go-to recipes when I'm tight on time, or if I feel like something a little lighter in the evening.

You know Spring has sprung, when you see fresh Asparagus! As we move closer to Summer, serve this chilled, over tender lettuce.

Asparagus Flavored Quinoa

- 1/2 lb. Asparagus
- 2 Cups Vegetable Broth
- 1 Cup Quinoa
- Cheesecloth or light kitchen towel

Lemon Vinaigrette

- 1 Tsp. Lemon Zest
- 1 Tbsp. Lemon Juice
- 1 Tsp. Dijon Mustard
- 3 Tbsp. Olive Oil
- Salt and Pepper, to taste   *I like White Pepper for this recipe.*

Garnish

- 2 Tbsp. Pine Nuts, lightly toasted

Lemon | Chris Liverani

Preparation

Wash and dry the asparagus.

Handy Hint Nature will help tell you where to remove the fibrous end of the spear. First hold the spear, one end in each hand, then begin to bend the asparagus into an arch. The spear will snap at just the right spot; no guess work involved. Repeat until all spears are free of their inedible ends.

Phyto Tip

Chefs, you know we don't throw anything away! Let's infuse our vegetable broth with delicious and nutritious asparagus flavor. Pour the broth into a medium saucepan. Add the fibrous ends, and bring to a boil.

While infusing your broth, cut the remaining asparagus into 1 inch pieces and set aside.

Soak the Quinoa for 2 minutes, drain and rinse.

Once you can smell the aroma of asparagus, remove the inedible ends from the broth with a slotted spoon and discard. Whisk in the Quinoa and cut asparagus pieces. Bring back to a boil. Then reduce heat, cover and simmer for 20 minutes. Remove from heat.

Handy Hint To prevent condensation from dripping into your finished grains, lift the lid and drape a towel over pan. Replace the lid tightly over the towel and allow to rest 5 minutes.

In a small bowl, whisk together all your dressing ingredients: Lemon Zest through Salt and Pepper.

Gently fluff the Quinoa with a fork. Spoon the finished Quinoa into a warmed serving bowl. Drizzle with Lemon Vinaigrette and lightly fluff again.

Sprinkle with pine nuts and serve.

Asparagus | Keegan Houser

Tina Martini

Phyte Bites

To date, Asparagus is our greatest hope in finding the cure for ALS, (Amyotrophic Lateral Sclerosis) or Lou Gehrig's disease. The phytonutrient, **Sarsasapogenin**, prevents motor-neuron cell death. It also is housed within inulin, a fibrous carbohydrate that lowers blood sugar due to the small intestines inability to break it down. This allows the nutrients to make their way to the large intestines, where it feeds good bacteria, making it a very effective probiotic. This combination of natural activity, makes it very effective in treating degenerative disease, i.e., ALS, Diabetes Type 2, and Chrohn's Disease.

The presence of four other phytonutrients, - anti-inflammatory powerhouses: **Kaempferol, Quercitin, Rutin, and Isorhamnetin**, give asparagus major cancer-killing abilities. I have used asparagus, with great success, in the treatment and complete eradication of Melanoma. Being very high in minerals and antioxidants like **Vitamins C and E**, it is, generally speaking, a great way to prevent nutrient deficiency over all.

Asparagus also contains a good amount of **Glutathione**; a combination of three amino acids combined into one molecule. This, many researchers believe, will eventually be the cure for Parkinson's disease. Rich in soluble and insoluble fiber, asparagus not only breeds good bacteria in the digestive/intestinal tracts, it also is a vegans best friend, as it is one of the richest sources of veggie protein.

The oder when one urinates after eating asparagus: **Sulfuric compounds**. This group of phytonutrients prevent hormone and digestive based cancers better than any other group of phytos. This odor lets you know you are digesting the nutrients effectively. This is about the only time stinky pee is a sign of good health! So, enjoy – the asparagus, not the odor.

Delicious Medicine | 37

Asian Shrimp Salad *Serves 4*

The dressing used in this recipe isn't really a dressing at all. It's more of an Asian-inspired pesto. We generally associate pesto with Italian food, but if you study different cuisine from around the world, you'll find a version of pesto in almost every culture. Use this as a delicious condiment for meat, fish, or vegetables of your choice.

Pesto

- 1 Cup Roasted Peanuts, chopped - *reserve 1/4 Cup for garnish*
- 1 Tbsp. Honey
- 1 Small Jalapeño Chili, *remove seeds and membrane*
- 2 Cloves Garlic, *peeled*
- 1 Tbsp. Fresh Ginger, *finely chopped*
- 3 Green Onions, *rough chopped*
- 2 Limes, juiced
- 1 1/2 Tbsp. Nam Pla (*Fish Sauce*)
- 1/2 Tsp. Salt
- 1 1/2 Cup Fresh Basil (*Thai Basil recommended*), Chiffonade *
- 1/2 Cup Fresh Mint, *Chiffonade**
- 1/3 to 1/2 cup Peanut Oil

Shrimp

- 1/2 lb. Large Raw Shrimp, with Tail
  I always buy shrimp in the shell. Cooking in the shell adds another layer of flavor.

Preparation

Pesto

* Stack basil and mint leaves, and roll into small cigars. Slice very thinly into ribbons. This is known as a *Chiffonade of Herbs.*

In a food processor bowl add Peanuts, Honey, Chili, Garlic, Ginger, Onions, Lime Juice, Fish Sauce and Salt. Pulse just enough to start to bring the ingredients together. Add your fresh herb Chiffonade to the processor. Pulse a couple of times, and then turn the motor on and stream the Peanut Oil into the mix until smooth. Too much processing and the herbs will turn black. Scrape into a bowl and cover, pressing plastic wrap directly onto surface of the Pesto. Chill the Pesto while you cook your shrimp.

Phyte Bites

Shrimp

Prepare some aromatics to place into your poaching water to add flavor to the Shrimp. This "*Court Bouillon*" can be as simple as carrots, celery, and onion. With our Asian theme, I suggest using Ginger, Garlic, Green Onion and Lime, or any citrus you may have on hand.

Prepare the poaching water in a large high-sided sauté pan. Rough chop the aromatics you have selected. First squeeze the citrus juice into poaching water, then drop the fruit into the water. Bring the water to a high simmer to release all the aromatic flavors. Then turn fire to low and add the shrimp.

Chefs, remember, poaching is a gentle process. Cook shrimp uncovered 5 minutes, or until shells turn pink. All protein continues to cook if it isn't quick chilled. Plan for carry-over cooking time since we are not ice bathing the finished shrimp.

Spread hot shrimp in a single layer on a sheet pan and cool enough to peel and clean. When ready, remove shells completely, including tails. Next, clean digestive tract using a pointed paring knife to lift tract out.

Chop shrimp into generous bite-sized pieces and gently fold chopped shrimp into your pesto. Lightly coat using a rubber spatula. Do not over-mix. Chill thoroughly.

When ready for service, sprinkle the salad with reserved peanuts.

Shrimp has a reputation for being high in cholesterol and is often considered an indulgent food, however this gift from the sea has lots of other benefits which can outweigh those concerns. Shrimp are high in protein, very low in fat, and contain good omega-3 fats which can actually help lower your cholesterol. The pink you see when the shrimp is cooked is **Astaxanthin**, *a very powerful antioxidant that helps sweep toxins from the body.* Selenium is also an important mineral found in shrimp that helps slow the aging clock. **Resveratrol** *in peanuts is also valued for its anti-aging properties.*

The remainder of our ingredients are superstars in eliminating inflammation. **Basil** *really helps our joints stay healthy and flexible.* **Ginger** *in particular assists in the healing of inflammation, as well as calming spider veins. In fact, there are so many benefits to Ginger that if I listed them all I wouldn't have room for anything else.*

Fish Sauce *is our most interesting item on the shopping list. Most of us link fish sauce to Asian cuisine exclusively, but surprisingly, it has a long history in Roman kitchens as well. With no way to preserve fish, salt fermentation was the only way to hold on to your catch. In Asian fish sauce, black anchovies and sea salt are used. This imparts the highly desired Umami flavor - the mystery flavor in savory food that makes us say,*

"OMG! This is so delicious!"

You could substitute soy sauce, but it won't be OMG!

Tina Martini

Jeweled Salad & Creamy Key Lime Dressing *Serves 6*

I worked for a corporate wellness company that would send me out to different locations to teach group fitness and **Healthy Cooking Lunch and Learns**. *I would prepare a health-supportive entrée in the employee dining facilities. On one occasion I was asked to create a salad that would visually wow, as well as pack the most nutrition possible - and top it with a creamy dressing. This is the result of that recipe challenge. The ingredients can also be worked around what you already have on hand.*

Salad

- 1 Head Bibb Lettuce, cleaned and dried
- 4 Radishes, thinly sliced
- 1 Each Naval Orange, Pink Grapefruit, and Blood Orange segments
- 1/2 Cup Pomegranate Arils
- 1/3 Cup Pumpkin Seeds, lightly toasted

Dressing

- 1/3 Cup Grapeseed Oil Mayo
- 1/3 Cup Plain 2% Greek Yogurt
- 1 Tbsp. Agave or Honey
- 2 Tsp. Lime Zest
- 2 Tbsp. Lime Juice
- Pinch of quality Salt

Preparation

Whisk everything together, then chill until service.

Handy Hint

To *"Supreme"* citrus is to give the fine dining look and palate experience that will garner you the Chef props you deserve. The knife work can make your presentation.

The citrus can be "Supremed" by first cutting off both ends, then removing the citrus peel with your knife, all the way around.

Very carefully hold the peeled citrus in your hand and then slice the blade of the knife along a white membrane, toward the center. Then slice it again across the adjacent membrane on the other side, lifting out the perfect citrus wedge. As you go around the citrus, fold the membranes back like the pages of a book. Now, you can move on to the next segment

Pomegranate | Feliphe Schiarolli

40 | Delicious Medicine   Tina Martini

Phyte Bites

Most researchers are convinced that the **Mediterranean Diet** is the best for overall health and longevity. This is primarily attributed to Olive Oil and it's great phyto profile, however I believe it's the inclusion of **Limonene** that has such a profound impact on longevity. Limonene is found in the pith of the giant Sicilian Lemons, which are almost all pith - and they are a big part of the Medi diet. Limonene cleans our cells, clears free radicals from our blood stream and tones our internal organs, similar to how exercise tones our muscles. This is the reason I have always recommended eating a small piece of citrus every day. And, be sure to peel it by hand, leaving the pith intact.

This recipe has a books worth of nutritive phtye. The Radishes, Pomegranate, Pumpkin seeds, Grapeseed oil, etc!

without the membranes getting in your way. Master Chef technique!

You. Can. Do. It!

Fine food is in the details, right Chefs?

Tasty Tip

When visual presentation is key, choose: *Supreme*. However, for everyday, be sure to hand-peel your citrus to retain the phyto benefits by eating as much pith as you can stand!

Tina Martini

Warm Spinach Salad with Coconut "Bacon" Vinaigrette

4 Appetizer Salads or 2 Entrée Salads

This recipe recreates the classic wilted spinach salad, only vegan.

The coconut "bacon" from the Chia Hot Chocolate recipe can make a savory appearance here.

Salad

- 4 Cups Spinach
- 1/2 Yellow Bell Pepper, cleaned and diced
- 1/2 Red Bell Pepper, cleaned and diced
- 1 Cup Cremini Mushrooms, cleaned and sliced
- 1/4 Purple Onion, sliced thin
- 1 Avocado, peeled and diced

Vinaigrette

- 3 Tbsp. Olive Oil
- 2 Tsp. Olive Oil for sautéing peppers, mushrooms and onion
- 3 Tbsp. Seasoned Rice Vinegar
- 1 1/2 Tbsp. Honey
- 1 Small Shallot, minced
- 1/2 Tsp. Dry Mustard
- 1 Clove Garlic
- 3 Tbsp. Pine Nuts, toasted
- Salt and Pepper

Preparation

Salad Strip large stems from spinach leaves by folding leaf in half with stem on the outside. Holding the leaf closed with one hand, pull the stem back with the other, removing the stem completely. Arrange spinach on plates or a serving platter.

Vinaigrette In a large sauté pan, heat 2 teaspoons olive oil. Add diced bell peppers and sliced mushrooms. Season with salt and pepper to taste. The mushrooms will start to release water. Continue to cook until all liquid is evaporated, and veggies are caramelized. Remove from pan and set aside.

Add remaining 3 tablespoons of olive oil. Stir in minced shallot and sauté until soft and aromatic. Add garlic, cook one minute. Add sliced purple onion. Cook 2 to 3 minutes to soften.

Keeping your whisk moving, stir in rice vinegar, honey and dry mustard. Whisk thoroughly and season to taste. Pour warm dressing over spinach. Arrange sautéed peppers and mushrooms over salad. Top with toasted pine nuts and avocado.

Phyte Bites

This is a heart healthy salad, as well as a Melanoma cancer prevention salad. All of the ingredients fall into heart health, sun damage protection, and eyesight protection.

Rather than a singular phytonutrient, spinach is very high in **Polyphenols** - a group of phytonutrients that enhance our immune function and contain powerful anti-inflammatory and antioxidant properties.

Mono Unsaturated Fat in the avocado stabilize blood sugar, and the **Carotenoids** from the peppers and **Vitamin D** from the mushrooms improve overall cardiovascular function. The **Quercetin** and **Allium** compounds stop environmental damage to our endothelial cells lining our blood vessels. This is important because we're only given a certain amount of these protective cells. The longer you keep your endothelial cells healthy, the longer you keep your heart in youthful condition.

Lastly, this is a big serving of **Vitamin C**. Another micro nutrient that gives our immune system the gentle push it needs to stay alert.

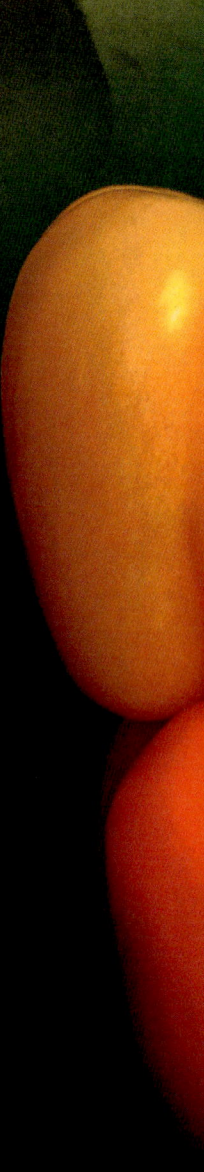

Tina Martini

Peach Glazed Salmon *Serves 2*

One of the most common questions I receive is, "How do I make a glaze that is very glossy, but uses no Cornstarch?" This prompted me to create fast, easy, and very shiny glazes from fruit preserves. Peach Glazed Salmon is just the beginning, Chefs. Try a Blackberry Balsamic Glaze as well. Choose good quality all-fruit preserves or jams.

As with all recipes, great ingredients are the first step to plating your masterpiece.

Glaze

1 Tsp. Grapeseed Oil
2 Tsp. Shallots, finely minced
½ Cup Orange Marmalade
½ Cup Peach Preserves
2 Tsp. Red Wine vinegar

Salmon

2 Peaches, halved and pitted
2 Large Navel Oranges
2 - 6 oz. Salmon fillets, skinless

Preparation

Warm the Grapeseed oil in a small saucepan. Sauté Shallots over low heat for approximately four minutes stirring occasionally, until very soft and translucent.

Add the Orange Marmalade and Peach Preserves. Stir until smooth and glossy. Remove from heat and stir in vinegar. Set aside.

Heat grill to medium-high heat. Slice Oranges into ¼ inch slices. Lay oranges side-by-side on grill, creating a "bed" for the Salmon fillets.

Pat fillets dry and brush lightly with glaze. **Place fillets on orange slices and grill 15 minutes,** or to your desired temperature.

Place peach halves on grill, cut side down, and grill 3 to 4 min.

Serve fillets with peach halves and extra glaze.

Phyte Bites

The big buzz around Salmon is the **Omega 3 fatty acids**. *These essential fats carry with them many benefits. But there is another nutrient that offers the greatest anti-aging benefits:* **Dimethyl-aminoethanol**. *DMAE*

This nutrient stabilizes the structure of our skin. It binds the water we drink to our tissue and keeps everything moist and supple.

Our arteries and veins must be flexible in order to carry blood efficiently. As we age, the tissue in every part of our body thins and loses structure. Foods like **cold water fish, Ahi Flower, Acai Berries, and Black Currants**, *just to name a few, encourages Collagen and Elastin production.*

This vital protein slows the appearance, as well as the effects of aging better than any skin cream could.

Balanced nutrition and a healthy lifestyle are your best tools in gaining entry into the **Super Agers Club**.

Tina Martini

Jerk-Spiced Turkey Burger with Mango Salsa *Serves 4*

Dry rubs are my "thing!" I love the deep flavor and crispy crust that dried herbs and spices impart to food. Dry rubs are any combination of dried herbs, spices, sugar and salt that you like. Jerk Rub celebrates the flavors of the Caribbean and is generally very spicy with the use of the native Caribbean chili, the Scotch Bonnet. I used cayenne and a mild chili powder blend here, but if you can find dried Scotch Bonnet, you'll truly transport your guests to Jamaica. Hang on to your extra rub, chefs! This recipe makes enough for two to three different recipes.

This bright fruit salsa can compliment many of your family favorites. Serving fruit with meat is an age old practice, as the enzymes in the fruit help break down animal proteins. The classic pork with pineapple is a great example. I like the cool mango flavor against the very spicy jerk seasoning. A hot-off-the-grill burger served on tender butter lettuce, and topped with the cool mango salsa... now that's a burger!

Dry Rub

- 3 Tsp. Dark Brown Sugar or Coconut-Palm Sugar
- 2 Tsp. each: Allspice, Thyme, Ground Ginger, Granulated Garlic
- 1 1/2 Tsp. each: Dried Chili Powder Blend, or Scotch Bonnet, Salt
- 1 Tsp. each: Cinnamon, Paprika, Black Pepper, Cayenne
- 1/2 Tsp. Ground Cloves

Turkey Burgers

- 1 1/4 lb. Ground Turkey
- 2 Tbsp. Tomato Paste
- 1 1/2 Tbsp. Jerk Rub
- Extra Jerk rub to season burgers while cooking

Mango Salsa

- 1 Large Mango, peeled, small dice
- 1/2 Red Bell Pepper, small dice
- 1 Small Jalapeño, seeded & minced
- 3 Tbsp. Purple Onion, minced
- 2 Tbsp. Cilantro, no stems, chop fine
- Juice of 1 Lime
- 2 Tsp. Honey
- 1/2 Tsp. Salt

Salsa
In a bowl, gently toss prepped salsa ingredients, and chill until service.

Phyte Bites

Turkey is packed with minerals, especially **Selenium and Zinc**. Selenium is at the top of the cancer fighting list. It is also considered a longevity nutrient, as it slows the aging clock. Zinc acts as a catalyst in our bodies: every time we eat foods high in Zinc, our bodies produce a very powerful antioxidant called **Superoxide Dismutase**. This is why Zinc has a reputation for building the immune systems response - it's really the Superoxide Dismutase that's been created.

Skinless Turkey is one of the best ways to prevent pancreatic cancer, provided the Turkey has been raised organically, and is pasture fed. This amazing protein source helps us burn body fat and induces deeper sleep. Turkey also has a very favorable ratio of **Omega-3 to Omega-6 fatty acids**. We always want higher Omega-3; Omega-6 is healthy, but too much, and it can cause malignant tumor growth.

All of the spices and herbs contain medicine too. After all, many of the medicines we're familiar with came from herbs. **Cinnamon and Allspice** are Mother Nature's antibiotics, they stabilize blood sugar, and lower blood pressure. **Chilies** open the arteries and are anti–inflammatory. **Thyme** brings a woman's menses down and eases hormonal discomforts. **Black pepper** cleanses the liver.

As you can see, all of nature's gifts have health benefits when used properly.

One additional nutrient is in the Tomato Paste. This provides the most concentrated form of the antioxidant, **Lycopene**, because tomato paste is cooked down to such a strong concentration. Two tablespoons of organic tomato paste per day is a great preventative measure against prostate cancer. Please be mindful of the acidity and be sure you find the right balance for your digestion.

Mangos contain **Beta-Carotene** which the body uses to make **Vitamin A**. This kind of Vitamin A is skin repair, reduction in sun damage, cancer prevention, and an immune booster. The **honey** is nature's moisture magnet: these two together are some of the best skincare we can eat! The bell pepper also contains those valuable **carotenoids**, high in vitamin A and C, they help us repair tissue damage, and move fresh oxygen out to the cells efficiently.

Cilantro contains **Apiginin**, this offers protection against Ovarian cancer, as well as being high in Chlorophyll. The green in plants refreshes the bodily systems, repairs damaged cells, and assists in the carrying of oxygen.

This is Delicious Medicine if you feel a cold coming on.

Preparation

Dry Rub
Measure everything into a small mixing bowl, or jar. Mix all dry herbs and spices together using a whisk or put a lid on your jar and shake it! *A little Zumba music, please!* Be sure to label and date the jar.

Turkey Burger
Mix all ingredients together. To avoid a tough burger, please don't over-handle the meat.

Form four patties. Put a dimple in the center of each patty. Sprinkle with a little extra rub on both sides, and grill over medium-high heat, 4 minutes each side. Allow the patties to rest 3 to 5 minutes, then top with salsa and serve.

Tina Martini

Stuffed Bell Peppers with Dual Filling Options and Sweet & Sour Tomato Sauce *Serves 6*

This recipe has two filling choices, and a sauce that works on all meat and non-meat dishes and is a winner for all taste buds and nutrition plans. It was created for a cooking class at one of **The LA Fitness** gyms, home to many semi-pro bodybuilders and fitness models. I was speaking on **Vegan Protein** and its benefits, and posed the age-old question from many a nutrition professor, "Who is the biggest and strongest in the jungle, and what does he eat?" The answer: The Silverback Mountain Gorilla. His diet is mainly leaves, bamboo, and grubs.

Plant based protein builds muscle. Needless to say, the Tempeh stuffing was a huge hit! And, we learned that the amino acids that build proteins are present in all **real** foods.

Peppers

3 Peppers
Most people don't digest Green Pepper well so I use Yellow, Red, and/or Orange peppers.

Sweet and Sour Tomato Sauce

15 oz. Can Organic Tomato Sauce
1/4 Cup Molasses
1 Tsp. Dry Mustard Powder
Any Mustard you have on hand will also work
2 Tbsp. Apple Cider Vinegar

Mom's Filling

1 to 2 Tsp. Grape Seed Oil
½ White Onion, small dice
¾ Pound Beef
½ Cup Cooked Rice
Any Veggies you would like to *sneak in* - small dice or shredded
1 to 2 Tsp. Vegan Beefless broth granules
2 Tsp. Garlic, minced
2 Tsp. Summer Savory, or Basil
The Summer Savory has a special flavor
1 Small can diced Tomatoes w/ Juice
1 Tbsp. Tomato Paste
Salt and Pepper to taste
½ Tsp. Red Pepper Flakes (optional)

Tastes Like Mom's

1 to 2 Tsp. Grape Seed Oil
½ Yellow Onion, small dice
1 Package Tempeh, crumbled
½ Cup Cooked Quinoa
1 to 2 Tsp. Vegan Beefless Broth Granules
½ Cup Veggies of your choice
½ to 1 Tsp. Italian Herb Blend, or Taco Seasonings, to taste. Adjust after salt & pepper
1 Small can diced Tomatoes with Juice
1 Tbsp. Tomato Paste
Salt and Pepper to taste

48 | Delicious Medicine Tina Martini

Colorful Peppers | Jude Infantini

Preparation

Peppers

In a medium mixing bowl prepare some ice water for blanching of your peppers, or you can skip this step for a crisp-tender pepper directly out of the oven.

Fill a large stockpot with water, cover and bring water to boil.

Cut peppers in half lengthwise, to create a natural bowl. Wash and dry peppers thoroughly. Remove stem, seeds, and membrane with a small paring knife. Place in boiling water for 3 to 5 minutes.

Remove peppers and place in ice water for 3 minutes to stop cooking and preserve color. Set aside, on paper towels.

Sweet and Sour Tomato Sauce

Place tomato sauce, molasses and mustard in a small saucepan. Heat over a low flame until it's the consistency of BBQ sauce. Approximately 25 minutes. Remove from heat and stir in vinegar. Set aside.

Cooking the Filling

Alright, Chefs, time to cook the filling and put it all together.

Preheat the oven to 350 degrees.

Heat oil in a wide sauté pan. Add onion and sauté for 3 minutes.

Add either the beef or crumbled Tempeh, and brown over medium heat. Add veggies of your choice, cooked grain, herbs and spices. Sauté for 2 minutes and add tomatoes with their juice. Cook until slightly reduced and thickened. Taste and season with salt and pepper, as needed. Set aside.

Spray a 9 x 13 baking dish. Spread a little Sweet and Sour Tomato Sauce over the bottom. Fill each pepper half and lay in prepared dish. Gently spoon remaining sauce over the top and cover. Bake 15 minutes, and then uncover.

Continue to bake another 10 to 15 minutes. Let rest 5 minutes before serving. Top with freshly chopped Parsley if desired.

Tasty Tip

If you find at the end of cooking, your food needs a little more herb and / or spice flavor, don't add raw ingredients on top of already cooked food. In a small sauté pan, add a half measure of the herbs and spices, in your recipes. Gently warm them for 3 to 4 minutes, to "Bloom" their flavors. Then, add a little of the prepared mix at a time: testing, and tasting all the way to service.

Phyte Bites

The first thing most diners notice about this recipe: the color! The more naturally occurring color on your plate, the more phyte.

Tina Martini

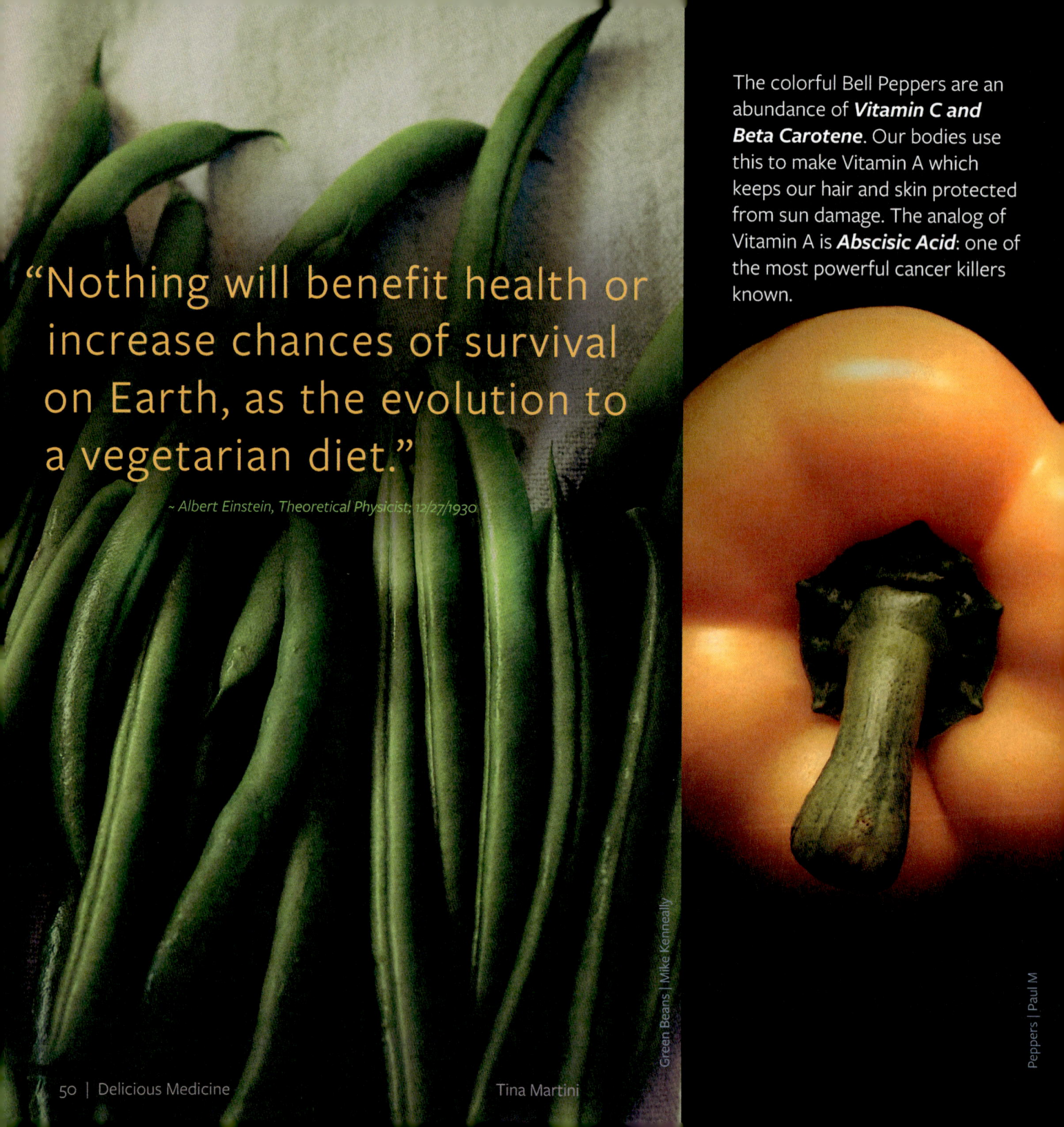

"Nothing will benefit health or increase chances of survival on Earth, as the evolution to a vegetarian diet."

~ Albert Einstein, Theoretical Physicist; 12/27/1930

The colorful Bell Peppers are an abundance of **Vitamin C and Beta Carotene**. Our bodies use this to make Vitamin A which keeps our hair and skin protected from sun damage. The analog of Vitamin A is **Abscisic Acid**: one of the most powerful cancer killers known.

50 | Delicious Medicine Tina Martini

Tempeh is made from a variety of legumes and grains. The fermentation process makes the phytonutrients more available to us. This is called "Bioavailability."

Tempeh is a great source of **protein** without the production of ammonia - a byproduct of protein digestion. That's why ingesting too much animal product is not recommended for radiant health. Too much ammonia can be damaging to kidneys, which negatively impacts other vital functions.

Do you have carnivores that aren't interested in vegan food? Add a little Tempeh to the ground beef. Everyone will get the benefit -

and you won't have to endure any, "I don't like health food..." grousing.

Beef has a bad rap.

But how much of it are you really eating? 4 to 6 ounces at one time is plenty. Beef is high in **minerals**, and we know nearly every disease can be traced back to a mineral deficiency. The most important nutrients to remember in beef; **Heme Iron** - the most usable iron, and **Zinc** that signals the body to produce **Superoxide Dismutase**. This nutrient is a powerful key to slowing aging.

Tina Martini

Mini Street Tostadas with Black Bean Hummus and Citrus Salad *Serves 8*

Here's another Delicious Medicine combination that gives you two recipes in one. And, this recipe has party written all over it! Use mini street taco tortillas, or use a biscuit cutter to stamp minis out of your favorite tortillas. For another fun presentation cut squares out of large tortillas.

Tortillas

Mini Street Taco Tortillas, or use a biscuit cutter to stamp minis out of your favorite corn tortillas.

Black Bean Hummus

One 15 oz. can Organic Cannellini Beans, ice water rinsed and drained.
One 15 oz. can Organic Black Beans, ice water rinsed and drained.
2 to 3 Tbsp. Olive Oil
1 ¼ Tsp. Ground Cumin
½ Tsp. Cayenne
2 Tsp. Chili Powder Blend, mild
¼ Tsp. Ground Coriander
½ Tsp. Lime Zest
2 Tsp. Lime Juice
½ Tsp. Lemon Zest
2 Tsp. Lemon Juice
Salt to taste
¼ Cup Tahini

Avocado Citrus Salad

2 Cups Chopped Kale, Herb Salad or Spring Mix

Vinaigrette

2 Tbsp. Sherry Vinegar
1/4 Cup Orange Juice
½ Tsp. Dijon Mustard
  Jalapeño Mustard is a also good
½ Cup Olive Oil
Salt and Pepper, to taste

Garnish

1 Navel Orange, peeled and cut into segments
1 Haas Avocado, peeled, pitted, and diced

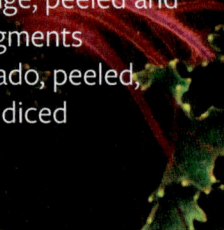

52 | Delicious Medicine   Tina Martini

Colorful Greens | Lukaz Szmigiel

Preparation

Vinaigrette
In a medium mixing bowl, add sherry vinegar, orange juice and mustard. Whisk together. Stream olive oil into the bowl, as you continue to whisk, creating an emulsified dressing. Season with salt and Pepper, to taste. Chill until ready to serve.

Frying the Tortilla Shells
I like to use a *no-flavor* Coconut oil. Heat the oil in a shallow sauté pan. The proper oil temperature should start to cook a test piece immediately. Place the little tortillas into the HOT oil, sliding away from you. Allow to cook 1 minute on each side, or until golden brown and thoroughly cooked. Drain on paper towels and salt lightly. Keep warm.

Black Bean Hummus
In a food processor bowl, blend room temperature beans, olive oil, spices, citrus and Tahini until smooth.

Assembly
Spread room temperature black bean hummus over crispy tortilla. Toss greens with some vinaigrette. Top tortilla with dressed salad and make it pretty with your avocado and orange segments.

Phyte Bites

Beans are a great source of Omega-3 fatty acid, the most talked about of all essential fatty acids. What we don't discuss enough is the **ratio of Omega-3 to Omega-6**. Too much Omega-6 can actually cause tumors to grow. For example, in our everyday foods we are exposed to processed oils more than we might think. The ratio of Omega-3 to Omega-6 in these oils are almost always out of balance. Even foods in their natural state can have an Omega ratio imbalance. For example, traditional Hummus is a huge food staple in our culture now, but Garbanzo beans have a very bad 24 : 1 ratio of Omega-3 to Omega-6. However, Garbanzos are naturally full of Delicious Medicine. The solution: just don't eat them every day.

Black beans have a very good Omega ratio, and when you look closely, they're really purple. Kidney beans come in white and red. Each color offers a different profile of phytonutrients.

All beans are great! I don't want to discourage any bean eating! My only message, as always, is eat a variety of foods so you are able to benefit from the natural variation in their phytonutrients.

Fiber is the real healer here, though. Beans contain both **soluble and insoluble fiber**. Fiber collects circulating estrogen like a sponge in the bloodstream. And we all think of one thing when we think of fiber: Yep! I'm going to say it, POOP! The estrogen is, uh, eliminated, (ah, a much nicer word), through our bowel movements. If estrogen doesn't hang around, it can't become malignant. Generally speaking, this provides great protection against breast cancer. Here's the kicker, if you don't clear your bowels at least once per day, the estrogen is reabsorbed into the body. To help, be sure to drink enough water always, but especially when eating a high fiber meal.

Sesame seeds, like Flax seeds, have shown tremendous results with regard to the prevention and treatment of breast cancer. High **Lignan** content is the primary healer here. Lignans not only balance hormones, they also protect hormone receptors from damage and are crucial in preventing tumors from forming.

Nature provides clues as to what the food is good for. Citrus is the shape of mammaries, and citrus **bioflavonoids** keep the breast tissue youthful in appearance and help maintain hormone health.

Hello men, this isn't just about "The Girls," or weird hippies living on veggies. We care about your hormones too. A long and healthy life means more great sex!

About BPA in Canned Goods
BPA is a chemical found in some plastic bottles and the lining of cans that can create confusing and incorrect messages in our endocrine system. For example, it is thought that BPA is one of the main contributors to the rise in infertility. When in treatment for a hormone-based cancer like breast cancer, it is imperative that you buy BPA free cans. It will indicate this on the label. That's why it's really best to cook dried beans from scratch, whenever possible.

Tina Martini

Tequila-Lime Chicken and White Chili *Serves 4*

My grilled tequila-lime chicken has always been a favorite, plus you really get two recipes in one: **Tequila-Lime Chicken and White Chili.**

Make the marinade and throw in either chicken or pork to soak for at least four hours. Then grill over medium-high coals just to mark the meat and get some smoky flavor. Finish your selected protein in the oven to ensure maximum moisture, while still enjoying the smoky flavor and beautiful hash marks from the grill.

Marinade

- 2 Limes, juice and zest
- Pinch Red Pepper Flakes
- 1 1/2 Tsp. Cumin
- 1/4 Tsp. Cayenne Pepper
- 1/4 Tsp. Ground Clove
- 1/4 Tsp. Ground Cardamom
- 1/2 Cup Tequila
- 2 Tsp. Olive Oil
- 1 lb. Chicken Breast, boneless, skinless, or Pork

Preparation

Marinade

Mix together marinade ingredients and marinate chicken or pork for 4 hours.

Chili

- 1 Tbsp. Safflower or Sunflower oil
- 1 Small Onion, diced
- 2 Cloves Garlic, minced
- 1 - 4 oz. Can of Green Chilies
- 1/2 Tsp. Cumin
- 1/2 Tsp. Cardamom
- 1/4 Tsp. Clove
- Two 16 oz. Cans Cannellini Beans, ice water rinsed and drained.
- 3 1/2 Cups Chicken Stock or Bone Broth
- 1/2 Cup Grated Monterey Jack Cheese
- 1 Cup Sour Cream
- 2 Tbsp. Whole Grain or GF Flour

Preparation

Chili

Heat oil in a stock pot and add onion. Sauté for about 6 minutes until translucent. Add the garlic, green chilies, cumin, cardamom, and clove. Sauté for 5 more minutes.

Add beans and chicken stock or bone broth and bring to a simmer.

Heat grill to medium-high. Oil your grate. Grill the marinated chicken breast for 5 minutes on each side.

Remove the chicken breast from the grill, cover and rest 6 minutes. Cut into bite-sized cubes.

Toss cheese with 1 Tbsp. flour. Wisk remaining flour into sour cream. Add chicken, cheese and sour cream to the chili beans. Gently fold to warm through over low heat for about 5 minutes.

Tina Martini

Phyte Bites

Omega 3 & 6

I have written before about the importance of getting the right balance of Omega-3 fatty acids to Omega-6 fatty acids in foods. **The Omegas in this recipe are in perfect balance.** Cannellini beans are a 1 to 1 ratio of Omega-3 fatty acids to Omega-6, and chicken is a 3 to 1 ratio, resulting in maximum anti-inflammatory benefits.

Also try this recipe with duck for a real Omega-3 power house. Duck and Goose fat are pure Omega-3 fatty acid. You see, when we eat too much Omega-6 we are actually causing inflammation. Researchers are connecting more and more diseases to the out of balance Omega-6's in our processed foods. For example, the use of GMO soybean oil is rampant in the food industry and this may be one of the main reasons we are seeing so much autism, clinical depression and infertility.

This is also a belly-fat burning recipe with the good fats being at the forefront. Safflower and Sunflower oils both burn belly fat without exercise.

The spices used are not only antibacterial, they also are shown to ease menstrual discomfort; particularly the cardamom. Lastly, the use of cheese and sour cream - both high enzyme foods - keep bacteria in check as well as promoting good digestion. These foods also prevent tooth decay.

All that in a little bowl of winter white chili. Another reason to eat a wide variety of foods every day to ensure we get all of the vitamins, minerals and phytonutrients we need without overdosing on any one nutrient.

Chicken

You must be asking yourself, why we've only included one chicken recipe in a book designed to assist you with your health. Let's talk about chicken:

Prepare yourselves.

If I could remove one meat from our societies eating plan it would be chicken.

Chickens are nervous birds by nature. To pen them up, one on top of the other, causes undue stress. This stress causes the mutation of the Progenitor Cryptocides Microbe. When you take a cross section of a malignant cancer tumor and look at it under the microscope, you will almost always find a mutation of the Progenitor Cryptocides Microbe in the tumor. This is not coincidence. Repeatedly ingesting the MUTATED Progenitor Cryptocides Microbe has been shown in many studies to cause cancer.

We all have the PCM in our biological makeup naturally. It's the mutation of the PCM, brought on by unchecked bacteria and stress, that can cause many types of cancer.

Essentially there are only three types of cancer in the world: Genetic cancers make up 2 - 3%. That means Hormonal and Bacterial cancers makeup the rest. That means that approximately 97% of all cancers are environmental.

This is great news, because it also means we can do something about it!

Please, do your best to buy only organic chicken. Embrace new sources of proteins, and focus on eating plant proteins whenever possible.

Tina Martini

A Celebration of Nuts, Seeds and Dried Fruit

Nuts and Seeds

The natural fat in nuts has a positive effect on our health and continues to be studied by top researchers. A great wealth of nuts and seeds exist so we can eat a wide variety very easily and in a surprising number of preparations.

Raw nuts and seeds have excellent nutritional value, but toasted nuts taste best in most recipes.

Dried Fruit

Dried fruit is always a great snack choice, especially since it's become easy to find good quality dried fruit that doesn't contain sulfite preservatives. The nutrients in dried fruit are concentrated due to the removal of the water, and in most examples, they contain more phytonutrients than fresh fruits.

Cherries and Acai Berries are very high on the *ORAC scale, but wild blueberries are right up there too.

Experiment with freeze dried fruit to add crunch and intense flavor to savory and sweet dishes. Powder freeze-dried fruit and sprinkle it on the plate; suddenly you're a *Molecular Gastronomer*.

Again, variety in our food choice is the best way to ensure we are getting all of the micro, macro, and phytonutrients we need.

Oxygen Radical Absorbance Capacity - a lab test calculating "total antioxidant capacity" of food.

Handy Hint

To impart the flavor of toasted nuts with the health benefits of raw nuts, grab a jar with a lid, a sheet pan with parchment paper, and preheat the oven to 350 degrees.

Pour half the raw nuts into the jar and set aside.

Spread the remaining nuts on the parchment lined sheet pan and toast them in the oven for 8-10 minutes. After the nuts are toasted, pour them into the jar on top of the raw nuts. Close the lid and gently shake the jar, mixing the raw and toasted nuts together. Allow the nuts to sit in the jar for a few minutes to impart toasted flavor.

Almonds in Shell | Roberta Sorge

Delicious Medicine — Tina Martini

Oxygen Radical Absorbance Capacity

2010 FOOD ORAC SCORES - USDA ORAC, TROLOX EQUIV., MMOL PER 100 G

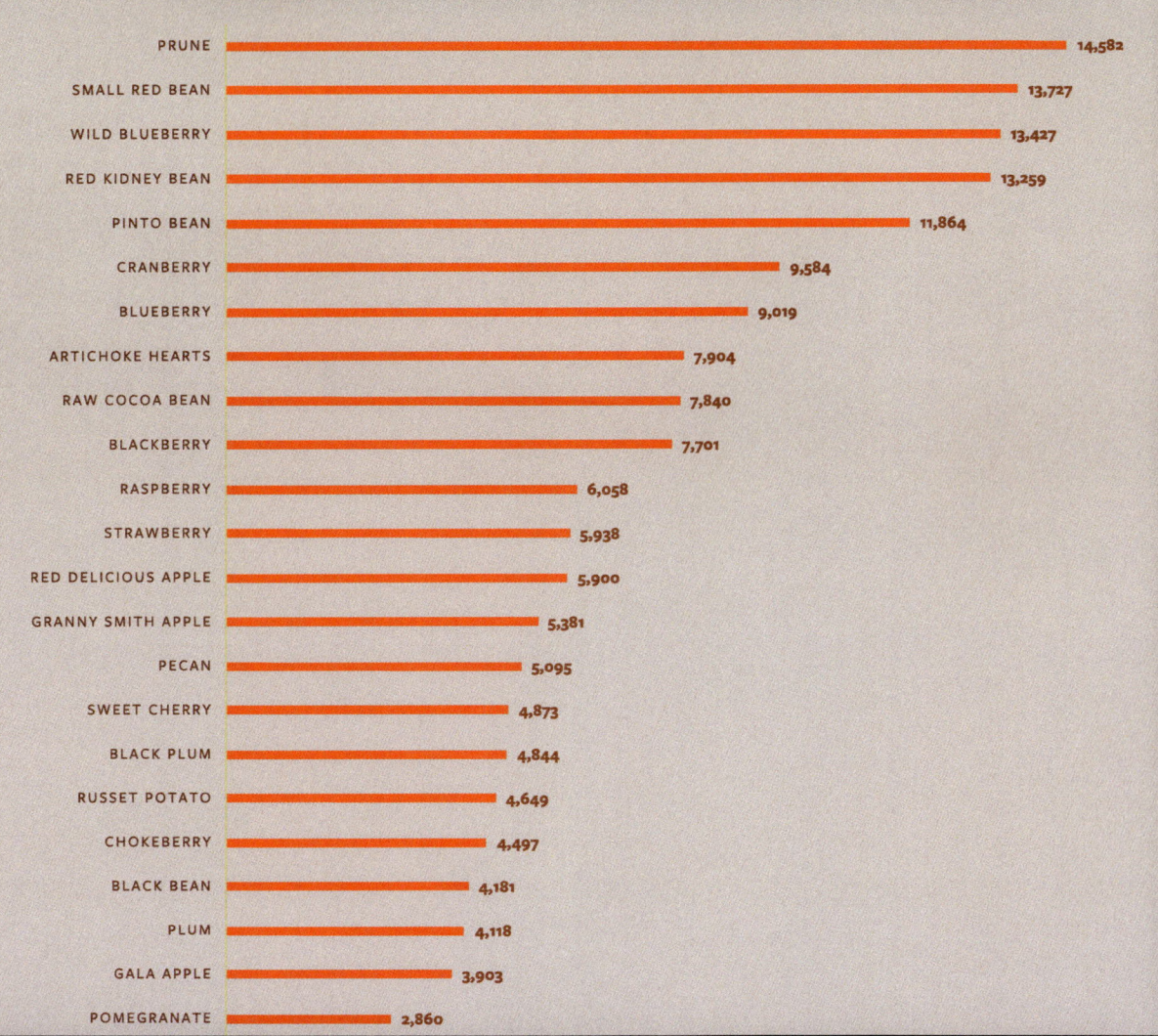

Food	Score
PRUNE	14,582
SMALL RED BEAN	13,727
WILD BLUEBERRY	13,427
RED KIDNEY BEAN	13,259
PINTO BEAN	11,864
CRANBERRY	9,584
BLUEBERRY	9,019
ARTICHOKE HEARTS	7,904
RAW COCOA BEAN	7,840
BLACKBERRY	7,701
RASPBERRY	6,058
STRAWBERRY	5,938
RED DELICIOUS APPLE	5,900
GRANNY SMITH APPLE	5,381
PECAN	5,095
SWEET CHERRY	4,873
BLACK PLUM	4,844
RUSSET POTATO	4,649
CHOKEBERRY	4,497
BLACK BEAN	4,181
PLUM	4,118
GALA APPLE	3,903
POMEGRANATE	2,860

भक्ति Bhakti Bites   Old Sanskrit: To Share   New Sanskrit: Love/Devotion

Loaded with Phytonutrients, these little balls are the perfect after-training snacks. Our bodies naturally produce free-radicals after exercise. To assist in the elimination of these potential cell damagers, eat 2 or 3 Bhakti Bites and a tablespoon of dried fruit, like cherries or acai berries, which are at the top of the antioxidant scale.

Play with the combination of ingredients to create your signature bite. I've included three of my favorite no-bake recipes below. All of the ingredients were selected for their Phyte! Plus Bhakti Bites are an easy treat to have on stand-by in the freezer too.

Almond/Coconut Bite

- 1/2 Cup Almond Butter
- 1/3 Cup Quick Cooking Oats
- 1/3 Cup Coconut Flakes
- 1/3 Cup Mini Chocolate Chips - *Dark, vegan chips would be great. Use the cleanest product available to you. Ordering online is a good option.*
- 2 Tbsp. Chia Seeds, bloomed in 4 Tbsp. of water
- 1/4 Cup Honey - *For Vegan, use Agave instead of Honey.*
- 2 Tbsp. Coconut Oil

Tahini Vegan Bite

- 1/3 Cup Tahini (Sesame Butter)
- 1/4 Cup Ground Flaxseed, *soaked in 1/4 cup water*
- 1/3 Cup Cashews, *soaked in boiling water for 20 minutes. Drain before use.*
- 2 Tbsp. Dried Cherries, Cranberries, or fruit of your choice
- 1 Tbsp. Nutritional Yeast
- 2 Tbsp. Agave
- 2 Tbsp. Coconut Oil
- 1/4 Tsp. Sea Salt
- 2 Tsp. Hemp Hearts

Peanut Butter Bite

- 1/2 Cup Peanut Butter
- 1/3 Cup Mini Chocolate Chips
- 1/3 Cup Quick Cook Oats
- 1/4 Cup Chopped Almonds
- 1 Tbsp. Ground Flaxseed
- 1 Tbsp. Chia Seeds, bloomed in 2 Tbsp. of water
- 3 Tbsp. Honey
- 2 Tbsp. Coconut Oil
- 1/2 Tsp. Ground Cinnamon
- 1/4 Tsp. Sea Salt (optional)

Coconut | Tom Woodward

58 | Delicious Medicine   Tina Martini

Preparation

Preparation is the same for all flavor variations.

Place all ingredients in your food processor. Pulse thoroughly, and then run continuously for 30 seconds, or until smooth, but not liquefied. Press a small amount together to check if it's too dry. If the mixture won't hold together add more nut butter, honey, and/or coconut oil.

Form into a large ball and then press plastic wrap down onto the surface to cover the "dough." Chill 30 minutes and then roll into bite sized balls. Cover and chill until very firm. Store in an airtight container in the refrigerator for up to three days, or freeze for up to thirty days.

Handy Hint

The ingredients will blend together faster and easier if everything is at room temperature. Place unbleached parchment between layers of finished **Bhakti Bites,** when storing.

Phyte Bites

Good Dietary Fat

A focus on getting plenty of good dietary fat is important. Studies at Harvard University affiliated Massachusetts General Hospital are unlocking new information about longevity and "Super-Agers" who live past one hundred and take no medications or have any real history of illness. These people generally consume the highest diet in good fats, and **Lignans**, *like those found in nuts and seeds.*

Each type of nut butter and seed contain a different phyto benefit profile. That's why I remind you to eat a wide variety of foods every day.

Using **Tahini** *(Sesame Butter) as an everyday ingredient in salad dressings, desserts and as a binder in non-meat preparations shouldn't be overlooked. One key benefit we receive from* **Sesame** *seeds: healthier, more flexible knees. Currently science doesn't understand exactly why Sesame targets the knees, but studies show that it does!*

Hemp Seeds *are rich in healthy fats and essential fatty acids, high in protein and contain high amounts of Vitamin E, phosphorus, potassium, sodium, magnesium, sulfur, calcium, iron and zinc, and essential fatty acids and contain no THC (tetrahydrocannabinol).*

Dehydration and Myocardial Infarction (Heart Attack)

Proper hydration is at the forefront of any solid nutrition practice. Many of the ingredients in Bhakti Bites protect against fluid loss, the first line of defense against dehydration.

The common belief is that plaque in the arteries is the main cause of heart attacks. However, plaque is natural and harmless, as long as it remains flexible. Chronic and acute dehydration make us crunchy and causes the arteries to seize, causing a plaque bubble to burst. The sticky, gooey center of the plaque bubble can block blood flow. The resulting chain reaction begins with chronic dehydration. Therefore, dehydration is the number one cause of cardiac related emergencies and heart attacks. According to the CDC, proper hydration also helps prevent unclear thinking, mood swings, constipation and kidney stones.

Too often people are training too hard, creating oxidative cell damage. It all goes back to dehydration. It's one of the reasons I created my "Gentle Cycling" program which helps prevent heart attacks after strenuous biking activity.

Instead of drinking more water and washing away valuable mineral stores, which in turn, create a cardio imbalance, we need a balance of high-water foods, essential fatty acids, proper, scheduled recovery, and an intentional return to Homeostasis - another reason to power down 90 minutes before bed. Meditating on the flame of a candle in a semi-dim room, deepening sleep chemistry, slowing the aging clock, and preparing the body to activate the healing response while sleeping.

Lying on one's left side for the majority of the night also helps digestion and is important as well.

Tina Martini

Nut and Seed Creams
Sweet & Savory Cashew

Originally used as topical beauty treatments, nut and seed creams have been around for hundreds of years. Now, with so many people unable to enjoy dairy for a variety of reasons, nut and seed creams are becoming superstars of the healthy eating movement. Cashew Cream is so trendy right now - and this delicious treat really does deserve its own trend. It's the perfect dairy-free addition to create rich dips, soups or sauces, or a delicious topping for any dessert that normally calls for whipped cream.

The Cashew tree is a beautiful being. This fruit is too delicate to export so one must travel to exotic places to experience the Cashew Apple, which is used to make a refreshing drink. However, the nut can be preserved easily and is a new focus of nutritional researchers. There is magic in the Cashew.

Sweet Cashew Cream

1 Cup Raw Cashews
1/2 Cup Water, plus water needed for soaking cashews
1-2 Tsp. Maple Syrup, or sweetener of your choice
1/2 Tsp. Vanilla
Pinch of finishing salt - *Maldon, Celtic or Fleur de Sel*

Savory Cashew Cream

1 Cup Raw Cashews
1/2 Cup Water, plus water needed for soaking cashews
2 Tsp. Lemon Juice
2 Tsp. Nutritional Yeast
1/2 Tsp. Minced Garlic
Salt and Pepper, to taste

Preparation

Sweet Cashew Cream
Place Cashews into a medium mixing bowl. Cover with water by at least two inches. Soak nuts for 4 hours. Drain water and rinse nuts thoroughly.

Place all listed ingredients into a blender. Start blender on *chop* setting and gradually increase speed to high. Allow motor to run until the Cashews are completely smooth. Place finished cream into a jar and use within three days.

Savory Cashew Cream
Follow previous instructions with Savory ingredients. Use as a sauce or binding agent in your favorite **vegan and gluten free recipes.**

Tasty Tip
Add Curry paste or powder, 1/2 Chipotle pepper, or any combination of raw veggies and herbs, according to your taste.

By doubling the amount of Nutritional Yeast, your end result will be a vegan "Cheese" flavored sauce. Fantastic over steamed or roasted veggies!

Cashew Flower | Shirankallu Sathwik Shastry

Who needs whipped cream, when you can have Cashew Cream!

Phyte Bites

Cashews are a Drupe fruit, with a firm seed inside a shell, like the Coconut, and are packed with minerals, particularly **Magnesium** and **Manganese**. These minerals are craving crushers! If you are having a craving for greasy foods, and/or sugar, it's generally due to a deficiency in these minerals.

Grab 1/4 cup Cashews, and the craving - unless it's a "head" craving, i.e., stress, fatigue, loneliness, or boredom - will generally stop.

Cashews are also a good source of **Selenium, Copper, and Zinc**. These minerals are antioxidant cofactors helping the body produce very powerful antioxidants from the food we eat. *Selenium* is a cofactor for **Glutathione**; excellent for keeping our nervous system healthy. This helps prevent such diseases as Parkinson's and ALS, A.K.A., Lou Gehrig's disease. *Copper* and *Zinc* are the cofactors to the production of **Superoxide Dismutase**, a powerful anti-aging antioxidant that also ensures proper growth and function of every bodily system. Cashews also protect us from heart disease and with a small amount of **Zeaxanthin**, our eyes are less likely to develop macular degeneration. Cashews are also high in **B vitamins**, another stress manager.

Tina Martini

Cashew Cream Mini Frozen "Cheesecake"

Cheesecake is definitely at the top of the list when it comes to dessert favorites. But so many people are choosing to give up dessert because it has a reputation for causing weight gain, addicting us to sugar and being too high in calories. This "cheesecake" recipe, however, was created for my cooking groups and has become a favorite of vegans and non-vegans alike. Making them in a mini-muffin pan makes portion control a breeze.

The key to successful nut-creams and nut-based "cheesecake" fillings: Soaking the nuts of your choice, **overnight**. Then put everything into a blender and process until light and creamy. You're the Chef! Use your creativity and combine what you have on hand to design your own signature cheesecake flavors.

Crust

1 Cup Packed Pitted Dates *
1 Cup Raw Walnuts or Nuts – your choice

Filling

1 1/2 Cups Raw Cashews, *quick-soaked* *
1 Large Lemon, juiced
1/3 Cup Coconut Oil, melted
1/2 Cup + 2 Tbsp. Coconut Milk *
1/4 Cup Agave Nectar, or Honey, or Maple Syrup (Vegan)
3/4 Tsp. Ground Cinnamon

Flavor / Topping Options

Salted Natural Peanut Butter
Berries – your choice
Caramel Sauce

Alternative Crust

3/4 Cup Oats
3/4 Cup Raw Almonds
1/4 Tsp. Salt
2 Tbsp. Coconut-Palm Sugar
4 Tbsp. Coconut Oil

Preparation

Crust

Add dates to a food processor and blend until small bits remain and it forms into a ball. Remove and set aside.

Next add nuts to food processor and process into a meal. Then

62 | Delicious   Tina Martini

add dates back in and blend until a loose dough forms - it should stick together when you squeeze a bit between your fingers. If it's too dry, add a few more dates through the spout while processing. If too wet, add more almond or walnut meal. Optional: add a pinch of salt to taste.

* Handy Hint
If your **dates** are not sticky and moist, you can soak them in warm water for 10 minutes, then drain. Pat dry to prevent the crust from getting soggy.

Lightly grease a mini, or standard size, 12 slot muffin tin. To make removing the cheesecakes easier, cut small strips of parchment paper and criss-cross them in the slots. This creates little tabs that make removing the cheesecakes easier to pop out, once frozen.

Next, scoop in 1 heaping Tbsp. of crust dough into each slot of the muffin tin. Pack it down with the back of a spoon, or even better, the bottom of a small glass. Really press it down to compact the dough. If the dough sticks to the glass, use a small piece of parchment paper to separate them. Then put in the freezer to firm up.

Filling
Add all filling ingredients to a blender and mix until very smooth.

* Handy Hints
For the **coconut milk**, scoop the "cream" off the top to provide a richer texture, or if the cream is already mixed together, just add it in, as is.

Instead of soaking overnight, you can **"quick-soak"** cashews. Pour boiling hot water over the cashews. Soak for 20 minutes uncovered, then drain for use.

Taste and adjust flavorings as preferred. If adding peanut butter, add to the blender and mix thoroughly until combined. If flavoring with berries or caramel, swirl on top of plain "cheesecakes".

Divide the filling evenly among the muffin tins. Tap a few times to release any air bubbles, then cover with plastic wrap and freeze until hard - about 5 hours. Once set, remove by tugging on the tabs or loosening them with a butter knife. They should pop right out. Keep in the freezer for up to 2 weeks.

You can set them out for 10 minutes before serving to soften, but they are delicious frozen as well.

Phyte Bites

Nuts are a powerhouse of nutrients. Cashews, in particular, are showing many benefits that other nuts don't possess. Though they are lowest in fiber, the minerals and antioxidant activity are at the top of the *Delicious Medicine* foods. Our eye health benefits greatly from a phytonutrient called **Zeaxanthin**. This powerful antioxidant is easily absorbed by our retina. The body then turns this pigment into a protective shield over our inner eye, thereby reducing our exposure to harmful UV rays of sunlight.

Toasted nuts taste the best, right? The newest work with heat application shows increased antioxidant activity. The higher the heat, the more medicine was released.

Tasty Tip
Cashews are the most versatile nut in the kitchen. Cashew Cream can take the place of dairy cream in almost any recipe.

Gluten Free Pizza Crust and Tomato Sauce

This is the pizza crust I developed for my GF corporate **Lunch and Learns**. I needed a crust that was fast and easy to handle. Gluten Free recipes are often unstable and difficult for a novice GF baker to execute. This ground flax seed and Chia slurry give this crust structure and stability, while maintaining a light, airy crispness. It also has the much desired "chew factor" that great Neapolitan-style pizza has.

Your family will say, *"Più pizza, per favore!"* – More pizza, please!

Pizza Crust

1/2 to 1 Cup GF Beer, room temp - *Use just enough liquid to bring the dough together.*

1 Tsp. Dry Yeast
3 Cups GF All-Purpose Flour
1 Tbsp. Ground Flax Seeds
2 Tsp. Salt
2 1/2 Tsp. Baking Powder
1/4 Cup Olive Oil
2 Tbsp. Chia Seeds
   Bloomed in 1/3 Cup Water

Tomato Sauce

1 - 28 oz. Can San Marzano Tomatoes
2 Tbsp. Tomato Paste
1 Tbsp. Basil
1 Tbsp. Oregano
1 Tbsp. Thyme
3/4 Tsp. Red Chili Flakes
   Optional, but very traditional.
2 Tsp. Balsamic Vinegar

This sauce is very herbaceous at these measurements. If you prefer a less powerful herb flavor, use 2 teaspoons of each herb instead.

Preparation

Pizza Crust

Prepare two rimmed cookie sheets with parchment lightly sprayed with olive oil.

Pour 3/4 cup beer into a small mixing bowl, and sprinkle the yeast over the beer. Set aside.

Stir flour, flax seeds, salt, and baking powder together. When using a stand mixer, a paddle will give the best results; otherwise use a wooden spoon to mix the ingredients by hand. With the mixer running, slowly stream in beer / yeast mixture. Add olive oil and Chia slurry. All GF dough tends to be sticky. To avoid a tough crust, please do not over mix.

Lightly coat a large mixing bowl with olive oil. Place dough in the bowl and cover with plastic wrap. Allow to rise in a warm place for 60 minutes.

When dough is puffed (it doesn't rise the same way traditional crust does) divide it in half. Place each half of the dough on the prepared cookie sheets. Brush a small amount of olive oil over the top of each. Press dough into desired thickness and shape.

Bake at 325 degrees for 45 minutes. Remove from oven and slide partially baked crusts onto a wire cooling rack. From here, crusts can hold at room temperature up to four hours or, when completely cooled, wrap in plastic and then in foil. Freeze up to one month.

When ready to use, remove the frozen crusts and top with sauce and other toppings. **Bake at 450 degrees for 10 to 12 minutes** using a preheated pizza stone or cookie sheet.

Tomato Sauce

In a large saucepan mix all the ingredients together, except the vinegar. Cook over medium heat mashing and stirring the tomatoes as the sauce reduces. Cook 30 to 40 minutes, or until the moisture is gone and the sauce is very thick. Remove from heat and stir in vinegar. Set aside until ready to assemble and bake your masterpiece!

Fresh Crust on the Day of: 30 minutes before baking, place pizza stone or cookie sheet in the middle of the oven. Heat oven and stone to 450 degrees. Top par-baked crust with sauce and toppings. Slide pizza onto heated stone or sheet. **Bake at 450 degrees for 10 to 12 minutes**, or until cheese is golden and bubbly.

66 | Delicious Medicine Tina Martini

Phyte Bites

Antioxidants

Herbs The herbs we're using are high in **Apigenin**, a naturally occurring plant flavone that acts as an antioxidant and exhibits anti inflammatory activities, antimutagenic and antiviral properties, and inhibits the proliferation of various human cancer cells, including breast, cervical, lung, liver, prostate, gastric, and blood-related cancer cells. I've also written about the research concerning its powerful effect on ovarian cancer.

Apigenin also calms anxiety and is showing promise as a protective agent for strengthening the brain in a fetus. There are many case studies linking a chronically agitated nervous system to clinical depression later in life. Omega-3's and Apigenin are critical to avoiding this in adults and children.

Besides our leafy herbs; flowers are very high in this phytonutrient. Specifically, **Chamomile** tea.

Mommies, please check with your OB/GYN to confirm a nightly cup of Chamomile fits with your prescribed regimen. Here's to babies that sleep through the night!

Tomato Sauce

Lycopene, a powerful antioxidant found in tomatoes, is the way to keep us from aging prematurely. It is one of the best internal beauty secrets we have, helping to reduce sun damage by as much as 40%.

Gluten Free (GF) Foods

By now, most of us have heard of Coeliac (or Celiac) Disease due to its marked increase in the mainstream population. Coeliac, is a word derived from the Greek word, *Koiliakos*, means, "to suffer in the bowels." For those with Coeliac Disease, grains and other fibrous foods pass through the stomach and upper intestines in their crude form causing great pain, acid reflux and indigestion in general. The resulting inflammation is painful and accompanies a host of other side effects that go along with being Coeliac. But it all comes down to the body's inability to break down gluten and other plant proteins found in grains. The primary treatment of Coeliac Disease is a gluten-free (GF) diet.

The three grains that are the highest in gluten are, Wheat, Barley, and Rye. Other grains such as Kamut, Durum, Spelt, and Farina are cousins of wheat, and can also cause irritation and inflammation as well.

Why "Eating Clean" is Important

Today, mass production of wheat, corn, soy and other foods has surprising health consequences. Mounting research starting in the late 1990's shows genetically modifying food to resist the pesticide, Glyphosate, has led to increased exposure to pesticide residue, causing an imbalance of good and bad gut bacteria, along with diminished vitamins, minerals and amino acids. As a result, over the last 20 years, there has been an increase in inflammation of the digestive tract and brain, along with an increase in Coeliac Disease, Autism, Clinical Depression, Parkinson's, ALS, Alzheimer's/Dementia, reproductive issues and Cancer.

National Center for Biotechnology Information: Samsel A, Seneff S. Glyphosate, pathways to modern diseases II: Celiac sprue and gluten intolerance. Interdisciplinary Toxicology. 2013;6(4):159-184. doi:10.2478in-tox-2013-0026.

Tina Martini

Gluten Free Flax Crackers

When I started my career as a chef, gluten free and other healthy options were not nearly as abundant as they are today. Although there are many good ready-to-eat options, making your own GF crackers is healthy and fun and can be very impressive.

Who thinks of making their own crackers? You do!

Crackers

- ¼ Cup Whole Golden Flaxseed
- ¼ Cup Ground Golden Flaxseed
- 1 ½ Cups All-Purpose Gluten Free Flour
  Plus more for your work surface
- ¾ Tsp. Baking Powder
- ½ Tsp. Baking Soda
- 1 Tsp. Coarse Sea Salt
- 2 Tbsp. Unsalted Butter, softened - or Earth Balance Vegan Butter or Coconut Oil
- 1 Tbsp. Onion of your choice, finely chopped or grated
- 2 Tbsp. Flat Leaf Parsley, finely chopped
- 1 Tbsp. Tomato Paste
- 2 Egg Whites, divided - or Vegan Egg Replacer
- ½ Cup Almond Milk
- Fresh Ground Pepper

Preparation

Preheat oven to 325 degrees.

In a mixing bowl, mix together whole and ground flaxseed, flour, baking powder, baking soda, salt and butter. Mix on medium speed until the ingredients resemble a coarse meal – about 2 minutes. Using a paddle attachment on your mixer gives the best results; otherwise use a wooden spoon to mix the ingredients by hand.

Pulsing the speed on your mixer, gently work in onions, parsley, tomato paste and one egg white.

With mixer on low speed, add milk, a little at a time. Mix until dough just comes together. Please do not over mix.

Divide the dough in half. On a lightly floured surface roll out each piece of dough into a square, about 1/8" thick. (Cover the half not being worked to avoid drying out).

Transfer the dough squares onto two baking sheets lightly sprayed with cooking spray. Cut the dough into small bite-sized squares with a pastry wheel or knife. **Fluted cookie or biscuit cutters can take your crackers to the next level.**

Brush with remaining egg white. Season with salt and pepper or dried herbs.

Bake about 15 minutes. Swap positions of sheet pans and flip the crackers. Bake until golden brown – about 18 to 20 minutes more.

Transfer to wire racks immediately to cool. This makes for the crispiest crackers possible.

Tasty Tip

Flavor your crackers your own way. How about Sun dried tomatoes, and roasted Garlic? An Asian spin: toasted sesame oil, green onions, and sesame seeds. You get the picture! Just keep the ratio of liquid to dry ingredients the same. The dough should feel soft and moist, but not sticky.

Handy Hint

Place your decorative crackers in a cute box. Add a jar of Vegan Walnut Pâté or flavored Goat Cheese Spread: You're the best gift-giver ever!

Phyte Bites

Overall, these crackers are loaded with Delicious Medicine, from the Flaxseed and Onions to the Tomato Paste.

Preventing Inflammation

Gluten Free eating is the biggest food trend the world has ever seen. GF shoppers can spend, on average, $100 more per cart. So why go GF? Well, for those with Celiac Disease, you may not have a choice. The gluten or protein in wheat and other grains causes massive inflammation in the intestines. Malnutrition can be a real threat because inflamed intestines are unable to absorb nutrients due to the swollen tissue. Others may have a milder reaction, experiencing bloating and other digestive discomforts. Research also shows the genetic modification of mass produced wheat and grains can confuse our bodies. As a result, our immune system senses an invader and, in an effort to eliminate the threat, responds with inflammation.

Heirloom Grain Alternative

In my café, The Ageless Kitchen, to make our breads and wraps we use heirloom grains grown from seeds without hybrid or genetic modification. Many of our clients with gluten sensitivity as well as Celiac Disease, reported no discomfort or flare ups. The original grain, produced on a small family farm and eaten in small amounts, enabled people who had not been able to tolerate grains for years to enjoy one of life's simplest pleasures: a slice of fresh baked bread, with house churned butter.

The Flaxseed

*Flaxseeds contain heart-healthy **omega-3 fatty** acids, fiber, and is one of the highest food sources of **Lingans**, a plant-based phytoestrogen that acts similarly to the hormone estrogen. You will notice I call for **both ground and whole seeds** since the seeds must be ground before our bodies can uptake the nutrients contained in the seed, while the whole seed acts as an intestinal broom, cleaning off the internal walls, making our nutrient absorption capacity more efficient.*

Being a phytoestrogen, men should not eat large amounts of Flaxseed. Small, infrequent amounts can still protect our heart health.

Tina Martini

Garden Flavored Goat Cheeses

Here is some fun fast food that the kids can help create. Who doesn't like smushing things in the kitchen?

Garden Goat Cheese

2 oz. Goat Cheese
1 1/2 Tsp. Milk - Your choice, i.e., unsweetened almond, goat, or hemp milk.
1/3 Cup Diced Tomatoes, seeds removed.
Fresh chives, chopped.
Salt and pepper to taste.

GF Tasty Tip

For a good ready-to-go baked cracker I recommend **Milton's Gluten-Free Multi Grain** with toasted white and black sesame and poppy seeds.

Preparation

Mix the ingredients in a small bowl until smooth and the ingredients are thoroughly worked through the cheese. If you don't have a piping bag, squeeze onto crackers through the corner of a sandwich bag. (Seriously, I wasn't expecting you to have a piping bag.) Garnish with a sprig of chive or slice of fruit.

Very Berry Goat Cheese

Mash strawberries, or berries of your choice, into the cheese and serve on whole grain graham crackers or whole grain bagels.

Tina Martini

Pineapple/Cucumber Granita *Serves 8*

Granita is the Italian word for fruit-ice. It's really an elegant Slushy dessert traditionally made from fruit and water, blended and frozen until icy, flaked with a fork and then re-frozen and served. However, Granitas can be created with almost any ingredients. When I was traveling through Italy I had a Red Wine Granita with wood fire roasted Grapes!

I think you'll find our Pineapple/Cucumber Granita the perfect treat to stay cool!

Simple Syrup

3/4 Cup Water
1/3 Cup Honey
15 Mint leaves
I have Pineapple Mint in my garden, so I use that, but any Mint is good.

Granita

1 1/2 Cup Pineapple, *peel, core and rough chop*
2 Persian (Baby) Cucumbers, *remove ends and cut into large cubes*
1/2 Cup Pineapple Juice
1 Tsp. Vodka (optional)
This helps prevent the Granita from freezing too hard.

Pineapple | Andra Ion

Tina Martini

Preparation

Simple Syrup
Pour water and honey into a small saucepan and whisk together. Bring the simple syrup up to a simmer. Do not boil. Stir until Honey is completely dissolved. Turn off heat and add the mint leaves. Muddle the leaves with your whisk, crushing them to release essential oil. Set aside to cool.

Granita
Place all the ingredients in your blender, including the Mint infused simple syrup. Blend until all of the ingredients are ground into a frothy puree. When the base is well infused, strain through a fine mesh sieve into an 8 x 8 baking dish. Cover and place in freezer. Set your timer for 30 minutes.

Here we go!

After 30 minutes, stir the Granita with a fork. You are creating air-infused ice crystals by scraping down the sides of the dish and moving ice crystals towards the center. We want to create a smooth, "fluffy" texture and avoid sharp shards of ice on the palate. The more you scrape the ice, the "fluffier" your end result.

Repeat this step two or three times. Remember to set your timer every thirty minutes.

Chill your final Granita base a minimum of 4 hours before serving. I always chill mine overnight.

Granita is perfect as-is, or as a topping for grilled fruit, breakfast yogurt or a summer drink. Use your imagination!

Phyte Bites

Pineapple contains **Bromelain**, a very powerful anti-inflammatory. The majority of this powerful enzyme is found in the stem and core. Chew on the core to help ease the pain of arthritis.

Vitamin C mends damaged tissue and oxygenates the blood. **Magnesium** is also prevalent in Pineapple. This essential mineral is a great way to curb sugar cravings.

Mint | Marko Blažević

Cucumber | Kate Freedman

Tina Martini

Buttermilk Dumplings with Warm Blueberry Compote *Serves 4 to 6*

These dumplings with blueberries were one of my dad's favorite recipes. We used to enjoy it on Sunday as a special brunch treat. Strawberries and Blackberries work well, too. The dumplings are light, with the tang of a cheesecake from the Buttermilk.

Remember, no peeking! You're steaming the dumplings and sealing in the flavor!

Dumplings

1 Cup Gluten Free All-Purpose Flour
1 Tbsp. Coconut-Palm Sugar
2 Tsp. Baking Powder
Pinch of Salt
½ Cup Butter, Cold - Earth Balance Vegan Butter works well, too.
1/2 Cup Buttermilk

Compote

1 Cup Water
½ cup Grape or Blueberry Juice
¼ Cup Agave
1 Quart Fresh or Frozen Blueberries, or a mix of your Favorites Berries
2 Tsp. Lemon Zest
1 Tsp. Fresh Lemon Juice
Coconut Milk Ice Cream, or your favorite Nut Cream

Preparation

Dumplings

Stir flour, 1 Tbsp. sugar, baking powder and salt together into a medium bowl.

Cut cold butter into dry ingredients using a pastry cutter or fork.

Add buttermilk to form dumpling dough. Set dough aside, covered with a damp kitchen towel.

Compote

In a large pot combine berries, water, grape juice, agave, lemon juice and lemon zest and bring to a boil. If the berries are too thick, add a little more water or juice.

Gently drop dumpling dough by the tablespoon onto the boiling berries.

🌱 Phyte Bite

Blueberries are at the top of the *Delicious Medicine* list. Science has shown that staining cells with blueberries makes it virtually impossible for cancer to grow. The Purple color represents the presence of **Anthocyanins**, a powerful antioxidant that has healing effects on the urinary tract, slows the effects of aging - specifically sun damage, and is one of our greatest hopes in finding a cure for Macular Degeneration.

There is much research into the **Gut Microbiome** (the good and bad bacteria of our gut and intestinal tract) and all of its digestive functions. Quality organic **Buttermilk** contains enzymes that help balance the microbiome - the home of your immune system and the beginning of the nutrition absorption process. A plant-based diet encourages a variety of good biome bacteria and the small amount of fat in the buttermilk, as well as the digestive enzymes, helps to maximize nutrient absorption from our plant rich meals. Today people are living with so much pain and discomfort from stress-related stomach and bowel disorders. There is a huge market for antacids and digestive related medicines. Most dairy products contribute to bowel irritability and inconsistency, whereas a regular, small serving of Buttermilk can also help relieve constipation.

Food variety is also very important in achieving a strong and diverse gut biome. Goat milk and cheese are great choices, too.

Cover pot and reduce heat to low and cook slowly for 20 to 30 minutes.

Please do not be tempted to remove the lid before 20 minutes, and do not stir the dumplings.

Serve with Coconut Milk Ice Cream, or your favorite Nut Cream

v Handy Hint

No buttermilk? Staying with a Vegan nutrition plan? Use your favorite plant-based milk and add a tablespoon of lemon juice to the premeasured milk. Set aside for 10 minutes. Viola! Vegan Buttermilk.

Tina Martini

Close Blueberries | Lior Mazliah

Delicious Medicine | 75

Mulled Wine *Serves 6*

Mulled wine, like many other ancient beverages, was fortified with herbs, spices and fruit. The Romans used Mulled Wine to defend themselves against the cold of winter and the Greeks used fortified wines as a way to avoid food waste. Fast forward from the 2nd century to today: Mulled wine is a central part of my newest disease fighting protocol and is a great way to assist the body in reversing heart disease.

We know the benefits of Red wine, but, add ingredients like Citrus Zest, Fresh Ginger, Cranberries, Cherries and Whole Spices, and we multiply the medicine, and increase our benefits, exponentially.

Mulled Wine

6 Whole Allspice Berries
1 Tbsp. Black Peppercorns
2 Whole Star Anise
3 Cinnamon Sticks
One 1 in. Piece of Fresh Ginger, sliced
3 Large Strips of Orange Zest
3 Large Strips of Lemon Zest
2 Bottles Red Wine, 750ml or 6 Cups
¾ Cup Honey

Preparation

Mulled Wine

Place the allspice berries, peppercorns, star anise, cinnamon sticks, ginger and citrus zest in large saucepan.

Pour the wine and honey into the pan. Stir to dissolve honey, simmer on low for 1 hour.

Serve hot and garnish with a Citrus Wheel and Cinnamon stick.

Tasty Tip Any Fresh or frozen fruit may be added to the wine before serving. Or strain the wine and serve remaining mulled fruit over individual shortcakes or biscuits.

Delicious Medicine | Tina Martini

Mulled Wine | Hannah Pemberton

Phyte Bites

Red wine contains a group of anti-aging antioxidants called **Bioflavonoids.** These phytonutrients slow the aging clock and keep our skin youthful.

Resveratrol is also plentiful in red wine and offers 3 distinct benefits: Increases longevity, burns body fat (specifically belly fat) without exercise, and protects our vascular system.

The **spices** used are Mother Nature's antibiotics, and the **honey** is a natural **humectant**, binding the water you drink to your tissue, increasing hydration.

Fresh **Ginger** is one of the most effective tools to balance hormones, cleanse the digestive tract and colon, and eradicate harmful bacteria.

Like the wine, the citrus zest is also rich in Bioflavonoids. The most beneficial phytonutrients in the citrus family are **Naringenin** and **Limonene**. Both strengthen the immune system and increase longevity.

Chia Hot Chocolate with Coconut Whipped Cream and Coconut "Bacon" Sprinkles

Chefs!
This is medicine-in-a-mug with a side of comfort. If you have ever been to Italy, it's sure to remind you of their amazing hot chocolate, which is really more like a warm pudding.
Delicioso!

Coconut Whipped Cream

- 1/3 Cup Heavy Whipping Cream
- 1/3 Cup Coconut Milk
- 2 Tsp. Coconut-Palm sugar
- 1/2 Tsp. Vanilla

Maple-Glazed Coconut "Bacon"

- 2 Cups Shaved, Unsweetened Coconut
- 1/3 Cup Braggs Liquid Aminos
- 1/3 Cup Hot Water
- 1/3 Cup Maple Syrup
- 1 Tsp. Liquid Smoke
- 1/2 Tsp. Sea Salt

Hot Chocolate

- 1 Cup Almond Milk
- 1 1/2 Tbsp. Dark Cocoa Powder
- 1 3/4 Tbsp. Coconut-Palm Sugar
- 1/2 Tsp. Vanilla
- 2 Tbsp. Chia Seeds

Preparation

Coconut Whipped Cream

Chill the beaters and mixing bowl. Pour heavy cream into chilled bowl. Start mixing slowly to add air. Increase mixing speed to medium-high, turning bowl as you mix.

Stop mixer. Add sugar and vanilla. Continue mixing until cream is in soft peak stage. Slowly drizzle in the coconut milk. Continue mixing until your cream holds a firm peak. Cover and chill until service.

Handy Hint For pure coconut whipped cream, purchase a Cream Charger online or at a restaurant supply. Fill the canister with coconut milk. Secure lid, aim and squeeze the trigger. *Viola!* Vegan whipped cream!

78 | Delicious Medicine   Tina Martini

Maple-Glazed Coconut "Bacon"

Place all ingredients, except sea salt, in a small mixing bowl. Toss coconut to coat thoroughly. Allow to sit at least 30 minutes. Overnight is great, if time allows.

Heat oven to 300 degrees.

Cover two sheet pans with parchment paper and spray lightly with pan spray. Shake excess glaze off of coconut and spread in a very thin layer over parchment. Place pans in 300 degree oven and bake for 45 minutes or until golden and crisp.

Sprinkle with sea salt immediately upon removing from oven. Allow to cool completely. Store in airtight container for up to three days. But I promise; it won't last that long!

Hot Chocolate

Whisk almond milk, cocoa powder, and sugar together in a small saucepan. Heat slowly over medium-low heat, whisking frequently.

You want to heat and froth the milk to achieve the luxurious texture we're looking for in our finished product. When the chocolate is just about to boil, turn the fire off and remove pan from hot stove grate. Whisk, to cool slightly. Add chia and continue to whisk just enough to separate the seeds. Allow to rest 3 minutes.

Using a rubber scraper, pour hot chocolate and any remaining chia seeds into mug. Top with coconut whipped cream and coconut "bacon" bits.

Tina Martini

🌱 Phyte Bites

I have one thing to say about the medicine in this recipe: **Flavonoids** *and* **Lauric Acid = Brain Power**.

From the cleansing of the neuro-connections in our brains, to the blood vessel strengthening power in the dark cocoa powder, coconut and chocolate are a magical combination. And, I'm not just talking about taste! Every day we are seeing the successful march toward the abolishment of Alzheimer's Disease; cases of severe and long-term dementia being completely reversed with the use of coconut oil in the patient's nutrition plan. People crippled with traumatic brain injury are having their neuro-connections restarted. This research is very promising.

Almond Milk and Chia seed provide good Omega-3 fatty acids and Vitamin E. All reduce inflammation and slow the effects of aging. Particularly the aging that takes place in our brains. Depression - both chronic, and acute, are related to inflammation.

Good quality sleep has to do with our mineral balance and all of our star ingredients are high in the 18 essential minerals. So this really is a recipe for cerebral success.

Delicious Medicine | 79

BONUS

My 3 Steps to Disease Prevention

I have only recently started sharing my *Three Step Protocol to Disease Prevention* with the public. It's hard to believe that these three little steps can have such a profound impact on our health. This is the foundation of my work in healing late stage cancer. To date, I have assisted 508 people who were facing late-stage cancer to completely restore and maintain Radiant Health. Working with people who face their greatest challenge has been the most rewarding part of my career. Our bodies know how to heal: we just have to give them the proper tools and encouragement.

The following three step protocol has been used to assist thousands of people from all over the world in restoring radiant health. This is a lifetime regimen that sets up every bodily system for success in fighting all types of disease.

1

Pure Cranberry Juice Shots

Anthocyanins, the powerful antioxidant found in Cranberries, Blueberries and Pomegranates prevent bacteria from adhering to mucosal membrane tissue. If bacteria can't "set up shop," then it can't get a stronghold on your immune system and create disease. Anthocyanins also strengthen the vascular system, particularly inside the heart.

Drink one to two ounces per day of pure cranberry juice in the form of a "shot." Drink one shot in the morning and one around dinner time. If this creates too much acid in the gut, dilute with a small amount of water.

2

Healthforce brand Vitamin C Powder

Vitamin C oxygenates the bloodstream, improves toxin removal by increasing the efficiency of our livers, and repairs damaged tissue and trauma in the body. It also is responsible for stimulating the immune system. It can be more powerful than chemotherapy when used correctly, and without side effects or damage to healthy tissue.

Stir 1 to 2 heaping teaspoons into cold liquid of your choice, twice per day: upon waking, and again before three o'clock in the afternoon. Do not take after three: you may be unable to sleep.

3

Omega-3 Fatty Acids

Essential Fatty Acid from Avocados, Coconut, and tree nuts are very beneficial to our health, especially if you want to slow the aging clock and stay moist and supple. Omega-3 Fatty Acids could be the cure for Alzheimer's, heart disease, depression, inflammation and many other disorders, both physical and mental. Cannellini beans have the perfect ratio of Omega-3 to Omega-6. (Too much Omega 6 can actually cause tumors to grow). Garbanzo Beans have the worst ratio, 24 to 1. Grass fed beef retains its high Omega-3s, as long as the cows don't eat corn or soy before processing.

If you feel you need a boost in in Omega-3s, the **Ahiflower** is a wonderful source of protective fats and Lignans. You can find excellent quality Ahiflower supplement capsules, and the plant itself is very good for the environment as well. We always want to get phytonutrients from our real foods first, however, the Ahiflower is a great back up plan.

To get your Omega 3's as well (as your Dimethylaminoethanol,) eat one tablespoon of raw, organic Walnuts every other day, and three 6 ounce portions of wild caught Salmon per week.

Get Shredded
30 Day Rip Up Plan

We can easily become addicted to fat, salt, sugar, and chemical tastes in our food. First created for bodybuilders and others looking to achieve the "shredded" look, I developed the following nutrition plan to provide a quick cleanup of the palate and the digestive tract. The protocol is very specific and strict, and doesn't allow for alcohol.

I recommend the gradual addition of this menu to your weekly planning. Two days per week to start, then increase as you feel is right for you and your family.

Then, as you decide to make permanent changes in your daily habits, gently remind yourself: Self-discipline is not punishment. It is one of the most powerful tools we have to strengthen ourselves and help us to move forward in our lives.

Each of these steps : additional movement or physical activity, drinking more quality water, allowing yourself to be relaxed and happy each day - is a step in maximizing your life direction.

As you progress, listen to your body and hold your focus on wellness.

82 | Delicious Medicine

Tina Martini, 1988

Breakfast

Jaeger Bomb Smoothie or Chia Pudding Parfait

Late Morning Snack

Small Granny Smith Apple with 2 Tbsp. Nut Butter or Nut Cream

Lunch

1 Cup Steamed Cruciferous Vegetables: Cauliflower, Broccoli, Radishes, Cabbages, finish with a small drizzle of good Olive Oil and/or Fresh Lemon Juice, if you like.

Roasted Wild mushrooms with 1/3 cup organic grain: Quinoa, Millet, Red rice, Wild rice.

6-8 ounces Baked Cod.

½ Small Avocado w/ a pinch of good quality Salt

Midday Snack

½ to 1 Cup Raw Fresh Vegetables - No carrots or celery

½ Small Avocado

Dinner

Repeat Lunch

1 Cup Steamed Cruciferous Vegetables: Cauliflower, Broccoli, Radishes, Cabbages, finish with a small drizzle of good Olive Oil and/or Fresh Lemon Juice, if you like.

Roasted Wild mushrooms with 1/3 cup organic grain: Quinoa, Millet, Red rice, Wild rice.

6-8 ounces Baked Cod.

½ Small Avocado w/ a pinch of good quality Salt

Bedtime Snack

90 minutes before bed repeat midday snack, except the avocado.

½ to 1 Cup Raw Fresh Vegetables - No carrots or celery

Drinks

One gallon of water is 16 servings. How close can you get - without living in the bathroom?

Ease into the hydration increase. We don't want to hurt our kidneys and we do want to maximize our water stores without throwing our body chemistry off balance.

Plain herbal tea or green tea; I'm not a proponent of decaf because of the chemicals used in processing. Keep the caffeine to every other day.

Tina Martini

Inspiration

We hope this book has given you new insights into the healing power of food, how to help reduce your risk of disease and improve your overall wellness.

As the Chief Wellness Officer and Executive Chef, choose to enhance your life and reach your goals!

Enjoy everyday.

Be present.

Be content.

Tina Martini

Chefs Notes:
Yes Chefs, that's you!

Index of Recipes

A Celebration of Nuts, Seeds and Dried Fruit	Page 56
Asian Shrimp Salad	Page 38
Asparagus Quinoa with Lemony Vinaigrette	Page 36
Bhakti Bites: Almond/Coconut, Tahini Vegan, Peanut Butter	Page 58
Bonus: My 3 Steps to Disease Prevention	Page 80
Buttermilk Dumplings with Warm Blueberry Compote	Page 74
Cashew Cream Mini Frozen "Cheesecake"	Page 62
Chia Hot Chocolate with Coconut Whipped Cream and Coconut "Bacon" Sprinkles	Page 78
Cranberry-Orange Chia + Oat Parfait	Page 24
Fast and Easy Cream of Broccoli Soup	Page 32
Garden Flavored Goat Cheeses	Page 70
Get Shredded - 30 Day Rip Up Plan	Page 82
Gluten Free Flax Crackers	Page 68
Gluten Free Pizza Crust and Tomato Sauce	Page 64
Grilled Chilled Peach Soup	Page 34
Jaeger Bomb Smoothie	Page 30
Jerk-Spiced Turkey Burgers with Mango Salsa	Page 46
Jeweled Salad & Creamy Key Lime Dressing	Page 40
Mini Street Tostadas w/ Black Bean Hummus & Citrus Salad	Page 52
Mint Scented Pineapple/Cucumber Granita	Page 72
Mulled Wine	Page 76
Nut and Seed Creams - Sweet and Savory Cashew	Page 60
Peach Glazed Salmon	Page 44
Stuffed Bell Peppers with Sweet & Sour Tomato Sauce	Page 48
Tequila-Lime Chicken and White Chili	Page 54
Tofu French Toast with Cherry / Orange Compound Butter	Page 28
Warm Spinach Salad with Coconut "Bacon" Vinaigrette	Page 42

10.07.2018